CAPITALISM UNBOUND

The Incontestable Moral Case for Individual Rights

Andrew Bernstein

University Press of America,® Inc.
Lanham · Boulder · New York · Toronto · Plymouth, UK

Copyright © 2010 by
University Press of America,® Inc.
4501 Forbes Boulevard
Suite 200
Lanham, Maryland 20706
UPA Acquisitions Department (301) 459-3366

Estover Road
Plymouth PL6 7PY
United Kingdom

Library of Congress Control Number: 2009939378
ISBN: 978-0-7618-4969-8 (paperback : alk. paper)
eISBN: 978-0-7618-4970-4

To Lisa Doby,
Who Loves Capitalism

And to Penelope Joy Milano,
Who Benefits From It

Contents

Acknowledgements

Many people were helpful in the writing of this book. My literary agent, Holly White, as always, played a vital role in many ways. Judith Rothman, Director of Hamilton Books and University Press of America at Rowman-Littlefield, provided the author with an unceasing torrent of much-appreciated encouragement.

My good friend, Paul Saunders, contributed editorial feedback, as well as extensive knowledge regarding a broad range of subjects. Ryan Bilkie, a brilliant student at Colorado State University, with a luminous future, also provided editorial assistance. The remorseless Adam Nappi provided much-needed, highly-skilled technological assistance at a critical juncture of the book's gestation.

My fiancée, Lisa Doby, aided the author in highly-skilled, much-appreciated ways that will go unnamed — but at which she is expert. My beautiful daughter, Penelope Joy, Chinese in origin but utterly American, provides constant inspiration and endless opportunity to appreciate capitalism upon every visit to Toys 'R Us.

Finally, no book providing rational arguments in support of individual rights can fail to acknowledge the genius of Ayn Rand.

Introduction

My earlier book, *The Capitalist Manifesto: The Historic, Philosophic, and Economic Case for Laissez-Faire* (Lanham, Md.: University Press of America, 2005) presented an in-depth and detailed case for capitalism. It was a scholarly work, running to some 500 pages and filled with dozens of pages of endnotes and bibliography. It contained an enormous amount of information culled from the fields of history, philosophy, and economics integrated into a single sustained argument—and represented, in effect, "one-stop shopping" for capitalism. Any reader seeking a full, scholarly argument on behalf of capitalism is encouraged to read that book.

But the intelligent layman does not require such scholarly detail and may feel no need of it. He seeks "just the facts"—the essential points—presented in a simple, easy to read format. This book is exactly that.

The single most important book ever written in support of capitalism is Ayn Rand's seminal novel, *Atlas Shrugged*. In addition to presenting a brilliantly suspenseful story, it provides, for the first time, the critical philosophical and moral principles necessary to understand and validate capitalism. The reader is strongly encouraged to read that book. Regarding basic economic principles, the best primer is Henry Hazlitt's very readable *Economics in One Lesson*. Beyond the three works just mentioned, this book makes no further recommendations for additional reading. Someone interested in advanced study is referred to the endnotes and bibliography in the original, extended, scholarly edition of *The Capitalist Manifesto*.

Today, in 2010, with the federal government pushing the country remorselessly into socialism, the principles endorsed in *The Capitalist Manifesto* are needed more urgently than ever. For it is not merely against the barbaric totalitarianism of National Socialists, Communists, and Islamists that the principle of inalienable individual rights need be upheld; but also against the smiling, glad-handing, "hopeful" purveyors of a semi-socialist welfare-state.

The country's current economic crisis greatly strengthens the case for laissez-faire capitalism. The United States approached the laissez-faire ideal during the late 19th century but moved inexorably away from it in the 20th and early 21st; today, it is a thoroughly mixed economy, a farrago of clashing elements—part capitalist, part socialist; part freedom, part statism; part private ownership, part government controls.

In every case in a mixed economy, currently and historically, economic problems are caused by the socialist, statist element of the mixture, not by the capitalist, freer elements. Contemporary disasters of the housing market, the banking field, and the automobile industry are no exception; in every case, the first cause and prime mover of the cataclysm lies with governmental regulations and their pernicious abrogation of individual rights. In every instance, the abuses and ensuing calamities would not have been possible under laissez-faire capitalism. (See Part Three—"The Economic Superiority of Capitalism.")

It is virtually beyond belief that today some intellectual voices call for a move to full socialism as the solution to the problems caused by the partial socialism of a mixed economy. This is akin to calling for more germs for a sick man—and reflects utter ignorance of basic economic principles. Perhaps when it is remembered that full socialism means not the system of Scandinavian countries—they are, without exception, mixed economies similar to America's—but rather the totalitarian system of Cuba, North Korea, and the former Soviet Union, such voices will be vociferously answered by the supporters of freedom.

This book is in full, one-hundred percent support of capitalism, and repudiates all forms of the initiation of governmental force, whether in the economic or personal affairs of innocent men. As such, the presentation is neither balanced nor open-minded, if "open-minded" means the belief that all opinions hold equal cognitive weight—for they do not. Rather, the book is objective.

In contrast to a deadly contemporary misconception, "objective" does not mean "balanced" or "even-handed." It means "based in facts." Objectivity does not involve a cognitive equilibrium of fact and rational proof, on one hand, with unsubstantiated opinion, on the other. This book is open exclusively to facts and to logical argumentation grounded in them. It is because of its objective method that its content is relentlessly pro-capitalist, for in a given case the facts may be overwhelmingly, indeed entirely on one side of an argument; and no facts exist, and no rational arguments can be adduced, to show the life-giving superiority of statism.

The author has a profoundly selfish stake in promoting capitalism. As an American, he is freer than the other peoples of the earth—although not as free as were Americans of earlier, and, hopefully, of subsequent generations. Since capitalism is the sole system that implements and protects individual rights, he recognizes that his ongoing freedom—and the growth of such—depends on capitalism's continued existence. All readers, worldwide, who seek to preserve their own freedom—or more urgently to gain it—should recognize a similar selfish stake in understanding and promoting the content of this book.

A final point is that many of the great men in the history of individual rights and capitalism are heroes—and this book is written by an unabashed hero worshipper.

Prologue
The Primordial Struggle for Individual Liberty

THE ESSENTIAL POINT

Capitalism was born in glory, created wondrous advances inconceivable to men of earlier (and subsequent) systems, and was then savagely assailed by moralists and intellectuals, the very men charged with responsibility for the protection of human life.

In terms of political economy, unrestricted laissez-faire capitalism is the greatest good of human history—by many orders of magnitude—but was repudiated because it rested upon a revolutionary moral code. This code—of an individual's inalienable right to his own life—is a life-giving principle anathema to mankind's "Moral Establishment": the governments, the churches, the universities, and the educational systems. To such "moral leaders," an individual's life belongs not to him—but to the state, to be properly disposed of by the will of the people or the people's emissary: the government.

This death struggle of the individual versus the state is the greatest moral drama of mankind's history and, today, in 2010, remains the gravest moral crisis confronting mankind, both in the United States and abroad.

A proper explication of this crisis is desperately needed. That is what this slender volume provides, and it begins with the rarest and greatest of all historical events in support of individual rights: the American Revolution.

A STRUGGLE AGAINST TYRANNY

A French economist, writing of the great scientist and statesman Benjamin

Franklin, enthusiastically gushed: "He has torn the lightning from the sky; soon he will tear their scepters from the kings." Prophetic words—for the revolution wrought by Franklin and his freedom-fighter colleagues accomplished precisely that.

On April 19, 1775 "the shot heard round the world" was fired at Lexington, Massachusetts by American militiamen at 700 British soldiers advancing on Concord to seize munitions stockpiled by the colonists. The revolutionaries had been warned of the British incursion by the daring rides of Paul Revere and others and the soldiers found 70 stalwart "minutemen," armed and ready, lined up against them on the Lexington village green. When the troops demanded the patriots scatter, the minutemen opened fire—and the American Revolution commenced. The British returned fire, killing eight and wounding ten of the patriots. The British forces continued to Concord, where they again skirmished with the minutemen. A swelling number of American patriots, firing from behind walls, hedges, and trees, relentlessly harried the troops on their withdrawal, turning retreat to Boston into disorganized flight and inflicting hundreds of British casualties.

The Rubicon had been crossed, a point-of-no-return boundary transgressed, and there could now be no peaceful re-imposition of British governance on her insurrectional colonies. It would be freedom or suppression–and most likely death—for the "traitorous" rebels.

Indeed, barely a month previous, hundreds of miles to the south, lawyer and orator Patrick Henry had concluded a ringing speech on behalf of American freedom to the Virginia House of Burgesses with the stirring words: "The battle…is not to the strong alone; it is to the vigilant, the active, the brave… There is no retreat but in submission and slavery! Our chains are forged! Their clanking may be heard on the plains of Boston!...Is life so dear, or peace so sweet, as to be purchased at the price of chains and slavery?...I know not what course others may take; but as for me, give me liberty or give me death!"

What factors led to such dramatic, world-altering events?

Amidst the myriad specific and swirling controversies, one fundamental principle stands out stark and bold: The British government, holding steadfastly to the mercantile conviction that colonial commerce was irrevocably the property of the mother country, imposed a relentless and unceasing series of restrictions on American shipping, trade, and manufacturing.

As a *Boston Gazette* editorial in 1765 eloquently exclaimed: "A colonist cannot make a button, a horseshoe, nor a hobnail, but some sooty ironmonger or respectable button-maker of Britain shall bawl and squall that his honor's worship is most egregiously maltreated, injured, cheated, and robbed by the rascally American republicans."

According to British policy, the goal of American commerce, in short, was to enrich Great Britain.

For decades, the defiant and aggressively self-interested Americans had continuously flouted British regulations and, by all accounts, smuggling flourished throughout the colonies. For example, John Adams acknowledged that

British regulations on hats and iron were simply ignored in Massachusetts; the Molasses Act of 1733 was openly violated; American trade with the enemy—unequivocally prohibited—was ubiquitous during the Seven Years' War; and Rhode Island was compared by the British Governor of Massachusetts to a lawless haven of pirates and buccaneers.

It is important to note that Americans traded with France—Britain's blood rival for control of the New World—*before, during, and after the Seven Years' War*, flouting the mother country's attempt to claim American production as exclusively its own. America traded on the principle of selfish profit, regardless of any supposed "national loyalties." American individualism was already pushing back against the arbitrary constraints of European nationalism.

In reality, smuggling and black marketeering, under tyrannical laws that coercively restrict men's right to produce and trade freely, are economic actions in support of political liberty. America was never a land of compliant and supine toadies before authority.

Eminent historian, Charles Beard, points out that: "American business and agricultural enterprise was growing, swelling, beating against the frontiers of English imperial control at every point." The British government sought to re-enforce its authority; the American colonists refused to kowtow before King and Parliament; the issues were irreconcilable; the conflict widened across the colonies; the impetus toward armed struggle grew irresistible.

In Boston the fuse was lit and the powder keg blown.

It began in earnest in the summer of 1765 when a group of merchants and craftsmen calling themselves the Loyal Nine agitated against imposition of Britain's Stamp Act, a duty placed by the government on most printed materials. The group grew—and soon became known as the Sons of Liberty. Its members included journalists and printers who denounced the Act in print. The politically prominent cousins, John and Samuel Adams, sympathized with the groups' goals. In August, the Sons hanged an effigy of Andrew Oliver, would-be Distributor of Stamps for Massachusetts, then burned his property and ransacked his home.

The critical principle at stake was that of "taxation without representation." The colonists, who had no representation in British Parliament, insisted that Parliament, therefore, had no just authority to levy taxes on Americans—and that only colonial legislatures possessed that legitimate power.

By the end of 1765, the Sons of Liberty had spread to every colony. The Americans had little hope that Britain's government would heed their demand for diminished control of their lives. The expectation, rather, was that eventually the mother country would land troops and seek to re-impose its authority. Therefore, they established Committees of Correspondence between the colonies to coordinate integrated opposition to what they regarded as egregious tyranny.

By 1768, British troops were sent to Boston to enforce the hated Townshend Acts, laws designed to more effectively enforce trade regulations and firmly establish Parliament's right to tax British colonies. Given the tensions with the colonists, the British Colonial Secretary instructed his military commander of North America to send such "force as you shall think necessary to Boston." On October 1, 1768, the first of four British regiments disembarked in Boston. An armed clash was almost inevitable, as townspeople bristled under the military presence and repeatedly insulted the troops. On March 5, 1770, a crowd of civilians, ignited by a trivial dispute and perhaps several hundreds strong, pelted with snowballs British sentries guarding the customs house. Shots were fired and, ultimately, eleven civilians were struck, five fatally. Although John Adams acted as defense attorney for the soldiers and all but two were acquitted, the "Boston Massacre" symbolized the increasingly precarious grip that Great Britain maintained on her rebellious colonies.

The Tea Act of 1773 ignited another firestorm. Essentially, because of reduced taxes it permitted a government-franchised monopoly—the British East India Company—to maintain its monopolistic status at prices lower than those it had previously charged. The Company appointed in each colonial city specific agents or "consignees" to sell its tea. Colonial merchants howled in protest. Legitimate tea importers who were not the Company's North American agents were threatened with financial ruin. Merchants who had long smuggled into the colonies cheaper Dutch tea would also be severely harmed by the legal monopoly's now cheaper prices. Additionally, many colonists feared that if the British government could successfully impose a tea monopoly in the colonies, it could subsequently do the same regarding other products.

In all colonies but Massachusetts protestors were able to compel the consignees to either resign or to ship the tea back to Britain. But in Massachusetts, embattled Governor Thomas Hutchinson refused to relent. Several consignees were his sons—and he prevailed upon them to hold firm in the face of colonial resistance. By December 16th, three ships—the *Dartmouth*, the *Eleanor*, and the *Beaver*—stood at anchor in Boston Harbor, seeking to off-load their tea. The colonists stood guard, refusing to allow it. Governor Hutchinson stood firm, refusing to permit the ships to depart without paying the requisite duty. It was a stand-off in Boston. But not for long.

That evening, roughly thirty to one hundred patriots, some loosely disguised as American Indians, boarded the three vessels and, over the course of several hours, dumped their cargoes overboard, consigning forever the disputed tea to the depths of Boston Harbor.

Although such responsible leaders as Benjamin Franklin and others condemned the lawless act, and insisted that every penny of the cargo's value be repaid, the "Boston Tea Party" led to a predictably different result: in Britain, it hardened the government's resolve to impose control on its insurgent colonies. In America, it came to symbolize resistance to tyranny and helped rally support to the revolutionaries' cause.

In retaliation and in punishment, the British government passed a series of laws which were dubbed by defiant Americans the "Coercive" or "Intolerable" Acts. One, the Boston Port Act, closed the port of Boston until the tea monopoly had been repaid for its losses and until the British government was convinced that some degree of sanity had been restored among Boston's lawless population. A second, to the colonists even more outrageous, was the Massachusetts Government Act, which stipulated that virtually all government positions in Massachusetts were to be appointed by either the British governor or the king—and which severely restricted the functions of town meetings in the rebellious colony.

Prime Minister, Lord North, left little room for doubt regarding the British government's attitude toward its mutinous North American colonies. He stated eloquently before Parliament: "The Americans have tarred and feathered your subjects, plundered your merchants, burnt your ships, denied all obedience to your laws and authority; yet so clement and so long forbearing has our conduct been that it is incumbent on us now to take a different course. Whatever may be the consequences, we must risk something; if we do not, all is over."

Britain's policy was an attempt to isolate what it perceived as the extreme radicals in Massachusetts from the more moderate patriots of the mid-Atlantic colonies and Virginia. But the American response dashed the government's hopes within months.

The "Intolerable Acts" promoted significant colonial support for Massachusetts and led to the establishment of the First Continental Congress in Philadelphia in September 1774. This was a seminal moment in the history of North America—and of mankind. Representatives from twelve of the thirteen colonies assembled; they decided to boycott British goods, and, if the "Intolerable Acts" were not within a year reversed, to cease all trade with Great Britain. The delegates also agreed to a Second Continental Congress to meet in May of 1775. Critically, the representatives vowed that their colonies would support Massachusetts in case of British attack, meaning, in practice, that the shots fired at Lexington and Concord but months later embroiled not merely Massachusetts in open rebellion against Britain, but the overwhelming preponderance of the other colonies, as well.

The American Revolution had begun.

The War of Independence lasted for eight weary, bitter years and was won, in no small part, because of the extraordinary moral strength of General George Washington, wisely appointed commander-in-chief of the Continental Army by Congress in June, 1775. Washington, although perhaps only a middling military strategist or tactician, was a superlative leader whose singular accomplishment was to hold together an army, ragtag and battered though it was, and keep American resistance alive in the face of staggering obstacles and reversals. In brief, Washington kept an effective fighting force in the field long enough to win support from European revolutionaries and eventually from France, Britain's primordial enemy. Britain's long-time North American colonies, after the surrender of Lord Cornwallis at Yorktown, were now effectively free of the mother country.

The United States Constitution — and Its Principles

The War of Independence had victoriously concluded. But the Constitutional Period of the American Revolution had barely begun.

What kind of government would the new country have? Would the war for independence result in merely a new and indigenous form of tyranny—or would the infant nation guarantee to individual citizens the inalienable rights to "life, liberty, and the pursuit of happiness" so famously endorsed in Thomas Jefferson's 1776 "Declaration of Independence?" Across the European continent, monarchs and aristocrats still held brutally autocratic authority. Throughout the non-European world, individual rights, political freedom, and republican government were unknown even as ideals, much less as practical realities. Even in Britain, birthplace of the principle of individual rights, the hereditary king still possessed significant power. What type of political system would Britain's cultural progeny create in North America?

The ringing answer was formulated in a mere handful of years. In May of 1787, the Constitutional Convention convened in Philadelphia. The assembly included men of extraordinary intellectual gifts—Benjamin Franklin, James Madison, Alexander Hamilton, and George Washington, among others. Even with Thomas Jefferson and John Adams performing diplomatic missions in Europe, and Patrick Henry declining to attend because he favored a weaker form of national government, the Convention featured a dazzling array of political acumen. Again to quote Beard: "Among the many historic assemblies which have wrought revolution in the affairs of mankind...there has never been one that commanded more political talent, practical experience, and sound substance than the Philadelphia convention of 1787." The essence of the group's intellectual leaders was that *they were practical men of genius*.

One great achievement of the resulting *U.S. Constitution* is the ingenious way it limits the power of any individual branch of government by a complex system "of checks and balances." To consider but one example: although Congress alone makes the laws, a President may veto its legislation—but Congress may override a Presidential veto with a two/thirds majority. But the Supreme Court can abrogate any piece of legislation by declaring it "unconstitutional." Supreme Court Justices are appointed for life by the President—and must be approved by Congress—and both of the two latter are elected by the people. The goal—and, in practice, the effect—was to prevent the government, in total or in any of its parts, becoming a violator, rather than a protector of the rights of individual citizens.

In September 1787, the *Constitution of the United States* was signed by the overwhelming preponderance of remaining delegates. But it would go into effect only if ratified by a minimum of nine of the thirteen states. The ratification debate was vigorous in many parts of the country but by 1789 the Constitution had been ratified in eleven states. That year saw the election of the initial United States Congress and of the first President, George Washington.

One of the important objections raised by the new Constitution's critics had been that the absence of a Bill of Rights made it possible for the national government to assume tyrannical power and abrogate the freedoms of individual citizens—the very freedoms for which the War of Independence had been fought. The Constitution's supporters generally agreed and, in a monumental step forward in the cause of human liberty, the First Congress formulated and legislated just such a Bill of Rights in the form of specific amendments to the Constitution.

The First Amendment stated: "Congress shall make no law respecting an establishment of religion, or prohibiting the free exercise thereof; or abridging the freedom of speech, or of the press, or the right of people peaceably to assemble, and to petition the government for a redress of grievances."

In short, the First Amendment prohibited the United States government from instituting an official state religion and employing the police power of the state to persecute non-believers—and, related, established freedom of religion in the fledgling republic, the unassailable right of an individual to worship, or not, as he chose. In this, Congress followed the illustrious lead of Thomas Jefferson—for, in 1786, the Virginia state legislature passed Jefferson's groundbreaking Bill for Establishing Religious Freedom, which stipulated that all churches have the same legal rights, that no church may receive direct financial support from the state, and that the state may not interfere with an individual's choice of religion.

Decades later, at Jefferson's own behest, his tombstone proclaimed but three of his myriad accomplishments: he authored the "Declaration of Independence," founded the University of Virginia, and was responsible for the state of Virginia's Statute of Religious Freedom. The founders of the American republic, descendants of people who, in Europe, had witnessed first hand the devastating religious wars of the 16th and 17th centuries, well understood the monumental—and groundbreaking—importance of religious freedom.

Of equal importance is the guarantee of freedom of speech, of freedom of the press, and, by logical extension, of freedom of intellectual expression. An individual in the new country would be free to say, write, or otherwise express any ideas he held—and neither secular governors nor religious leaders were granted authority to restrict him.

This vital principle protected freedom of the human mind and it bore vast orchards of life-giving fruit in the centuries to follow—and quickly.

Prominently featured among the remaining guaranteed rights is the Second Amendment, which boldly states: "A well regulated Militia, being necessary to the security of a free State, the right of the people to keep and bear Arms, shall not be infringed." The reference to the security of "a free state" makes clear that the first Congress was thinking not merely of physical protection for innocent persons against criminals but, more broadly, of defense of political freedom against a tyrannical government, whether domestic or foreign.

The *United States Constitution* and its first ten amendments established the nascent republic as the freest nation in world history.

What is the essence of this pioneering achievement?

Novelist-philosopher Ayn Rand (herself an immigrant to America from the Soviet Union) explained it best: "*America's founding ideal was the principle of individual rights...*The rest—everything that America achieved, everything she became, everything 'noble and just,' and heroic, and great, and unprecedented in human history—was the logical consequence of fidelity to that one principle."

The one fundamental right is that of an individual human being to his own life. All other rights flow logically from this basic moral principle. Since the sustenance of a human life requires an on-going process of self-generated actions—for example, to grow food or earn the money to buy it, to build a home or purchase one, to gain an education or apply it, etc.—it follows that a right to life means the freedom to take all the actions necessary to the pursuit of personal fulfillment and happiness.

But, unfortunately, other human beings can potentially violate a man's right to his own life. By initiating force against him (or fraud, an indirect use of force), they can murder, maim, assault, or enslave him—and/or they can rob him of wealth, thereby curtailing or even expunging his ability to support his life. By undermining or outright terminating an individual's life, the initiation of physical force, in any of its hideous iterations, is evil—and honest men require protection from it.

That protection is provided by a proper government.

A morally legitimate government must be strong enough to protect an individual's rights—but not strong enough to violate them. Its specific powers and spheres of activity must be rigorously defined by constitutional law, and, by the same authority, it must be legally shackled from intruding into arenas appropriately left exclusively to private choice and initiative.

In brief: the government of a free society must respect—indeed, uphold and protect—the right of an adult individual to any activity that does not initiate force or fraud against an innocent victim—and it must vigorously police and prosecute every species of such criminality.

So, for example, an individual must be protected in his right to speak, read, write or shout from his rooftop any ideas, without exception—in his right to worship, or not, as he sees fit—in his right to own and develop property as he deems best—in his right to earn and retain wealth—and, more broadly, in his right to engage in every specific form of peaceable, non-coercive adult behavior, even including his right to self-destructively imbibe toxic substances.

To combine formulations from leading historic supporters of freedom: an individual has the right to life, liberty, property, and the pursuit of happiness; and such rights are "inalienable," i.e., they cannot be transferred, forfeited, surrendered, or lost.

In order to protect the inalienable rights of every individual, a government must faithfully perform—and be stringently limited to—three functions.

One is to provide a criminal justice system—a police force, criminal courts, penal facilities, etc.—to protect innocent men from those who initiate force or fraud. A second perhaps even more important, is to institute a system of civil courts to arbitrate legitimate disputes between and among honest men — of critical significance to day-to-day well-being and economic progress, because, to take but one example, the trust to enter contractual agreements could not exist in the absence of their upholding by law. The third is to establish a volunteer military in order to defend the nation against possible foreign aggressors — volunteer, not coercively conscripted, because the defense of a free society requires that society to be free. All other activities are to be left exceptionlessly to private individuals, private enterprise, and private initiative.

For example: the government's sole (indispensable and critically important) role in the economy is identical to its role in every other aspect of human life: to uphold individual rights — to protect the inviolability of contracts, to punish fraud, and to ban and retribute the initiation of force.

If and when the government attempts to do other than this, it morphs into a violator of men's rights, no longer a protector — and, because of its unchallengeable legal jurisdiction, the most powerful and dangerous violator conceivable.

So, to illustrate this point: an individual has the moral right to build on, improve, and develop his own property. But if the government, ostensibly to "protect the environment," bans an oil company from drilling or an individual from construction on their respective lands, the right of free men to dispose of private property in accordance with their best judgment is thereby abrogated.

Or: an individual has the right to sell or retain his property in accordance with his own values. But under the law of "eminent domain" the state has the power to seize private property for whatever it deems in "the public interest." That the government is legally required to pay the owner "fair market value" is irrelevant. The essence of the case is the government's power to legally coerce a property owner to sell regardless of his values or choices.

Or: A company has the inalienable right to hire any worker voluntarily willing to work for it and a worker has the same right to work for any company voluntarily willing to hire him. But if the government forces a company to negotiate exclusively with a union, and permits no such negotiations with non-union workers, it violates the right of both companies and independent workers to negotiate with, hire, and/or work for whomever they will.

Or, as a final example: a company has the right to sell as many products on a competitively open market as it can and, similarly, customers have a right to purchase as much of a company's goods as they desire and can afford. If the government legally breaks up a successful company that has achieved enormous market share in open competition on a free market, it violates both the right of the company to sell as much as it pleases and the right of customers to patronize that company to the full extent they prefer.

To protect such freedom in the economic sphere, a character in Ayn Rand's *Atlas Shrugged*, a judge, proposes to add a critical amendment to the *U.S. Constitution*: "Congress shall make no law abridging the freedom of production and trade..."

Another way in which modern governments, including America's, reject limitation to the three functions outlined above and, as a consequence, violate individual rights egregiously is in the establishment of a welfare state. Governmental welfare programs involve the coercive redistribution of wealth from the productive to the non-productive; in short, the government initiates force against honest working men and robs them to financially support those who are not working. In a free society, such institutionalized theft is rigorously, universally expunged; all charity is left to private individuals and organizations and to voluntary effort. No one is robbed or forced to support the indigent.

Capitalism is, in Ayn Rand's brilliant definition: "the system of individual rights, including property rights, in which all property is privately owned." Critically, the government is legally restricted from initiating force against innocent men.

Freedom, in its essential meaning, is to be protected against the initiation of force by either private citizens or the government.

The *U.S. Constitution* and the government founded on it were not and are not perfect. The *Constitution's* essential actuating principle of inalienable individual rights was never rigorously defined. Because of this failing, the document legally sanctioned, in specific cases, the initiation of force against innocent individuals, including by the government.

One manifest historic contradiction was the continued practice of human slavery. Although the 13th Amendment finally wrought the demise of that hideous institution in 1865, the document's fundamental imperfections persisted, making possible in the 20th century the government's initiation of force against innocent men in the establishment of a semi-socialist welfare state. America's greatness is that there, more than in any other nation, the government was limited to the protection of individual rights—but even there, it was legally permitted to devolve into a violator of them.

Nevertheless, the rights acknowledged and upheld in the "Bill of Rights" established America as the freest nation of history, represented a seminal advance in the primordial struggle for human liberty, and serve as inspiration for the freedoms men can attain in the future—both in America and abroad.

This principle of inalienable individual rights is the animating essence of capitalism, the core of its meaning, its nature, its glory. We can think of individual rights as the spirit—and the philosophy—of capitalism.

But this philosophy has been tragically rare throughout mankind's history and never more so than today, in the 21st century.

MANKIND'S HEARTBREAKING ABSENCE OF FREEDOM

The political status quo throughout history and continuing until this day has been, in a variety of forms, *statism*—the theory and system of government upholding the subordination of the individual to the state, the repudiation of inalienable individual rights, and each individual's unremitting moral duty to sacrifice himself to society.

Most political systems have ruthlessly suppressed the rights and lives of individuals. Feudalism, military dictatorships, theocracies, National Socialism (Nazism), and Communism are but several examples. What these and other such systems share in common is the utter rejection of individual rights. Whether men are forced to sacrifice for the tribe, for the king or aristocracy, for the clergy, for the race, for the working class, or some other power deemed superior to individual life, a human being has no sovereign moral authority to govern his own existence. He is the chattel property of the state.

In every political system of history except capitalism, properly defined, the government has the legal right to initiate force against its own citizens.

The horrors of such lack of freedom are historically and currently manifest.

Under feudalism, for example, the common man—the overwhelming preponderance of mankind—was suppressed by the *ancien regime*, the feudal aristocracy or ancient regime. Serfs were tied to the land in centuries-long involuntary servitude and, in practice, were indistinguishable from slaves. Commoners, more broadly, were utterly subordinate to the dictates of church, king and aristocracy, and dissent was brutally repressed. Heretics were burned at the stake— women were condemned to death for practicing "witchcraft" and mankind's most advanced thinkers were often executed, threatened with torture, and/or incarcerated for the "crime" of independent thinking.

In the late 19th century, European imperialists—overwhelmingly monarchs, aristocrats, and their political supporters—conquered large portions of Asia and Africa. They ruled brutally but in some cases at least built infrastructure, improved medical and educational conditions, and upgraded local economies, e.g., the British. When the colonialists packed their bags and went home in the years following World War II, local economic development generally ceased; all that remained was a vastly worse brutality. For example, China, North Korea, Vietnam, and Cambodia regressed into the most repressive totalitarian regime of human history—Communism—which murdered 100 million blameless victims in some 80 years, most in the aforementioned Asian nations.

At the same time, African states, ruled by an endless succession of dictators, whether tribal gangs, religious zealots, or blood-drenched "warlords," i.e., glorified thugs, permitted not the slightest breath of individual rights, neither in theory nor practice. These brutes imposed repression and murder of a nature unspeakably hideous. In Rwanda, for example, Hutu "militia" murdered 800,000 "tribal enemies," mostly of the Tutsi tribe. Generally, they hacked to pieces their victims with machetes—men, women, invalids, children, babies—and stacked the body parts in piles, like so much ghastly cordwood. To such primitive mentalities, neither an individual's moral character nor his specific achievements nor his innocence of criminal wrongdoing signified; the sole issue of concern was the tribe (or ethnic group) into which he was involuntarily born.

In Sudan, the jihadist regime in Khartoum, fanatically committed to spreading Islam by the sword, has enslaved and/or murdered—by conservative estimate—hundreds of thousands, probably millions of black Sudanese non-Muslims. In Somalia, unremitting civil war rages remorselessly between rival clans and/or "warlords" and/or religious zealots—and literally countless civilians, caught in the crossfire, are now corpses. With the principle of individual rights a cultural pariah, human life has scant value and—tragically—murderous oppression scant moral deterrent. Today, Somalia, lawless, blood-drenched, bristling with modern piracy, is regarded among chary travelers as "the most dangerous destination on earth."

In Europe, the National Socialists formed an infamous modern example. In Germany, the Nazis imposed a crushing dictatorship, then plunged the world into catastrophic war and butchered millions of innocent victims. Similar to their Rwandan counterparts five decades later, these violently maleficent bigots dismissed all considerations of individual life, choice, and merit, esteeming solely racial or ethnic membership.

Less notorious but no less lethal, the Soviet regime under Lenin and Trotsky, fully as much as under Stalin, engaged in an orgy of class warfare, exterminating "enemies of the proletariat" by the tens of millions. Communists worldwide, as a matter of unabating philosophic commitment, abjure the related principles of individualism and individual rights, recognizing in their stead only membership in ceaselessly warring economic classes.

During World War I and its aftermath, the Ottoman Empire—centered in present day Turkey—slaughtered roughly 1.5 million Armenians in a genocidal mania that presaged the Jewish Holocaust to come two-and-a-half decades subsequently.

Not to go unmentioned, human slavery has been a monstrous institution universally practiced throughout history—and one continuing in the 21st century. Slavery was common on every inhabited continent for thousands of years. Its practice pre-dated the founding of Buddhism, Christianity, and Islam. The Roman and Ottoman empires were but two examples of vast slave-driving imperial systems. The very English word "slave" is a derivative of the name "Slav," because Slavic peoples (eastern and central Europeans) were enslaved on such a massive scale, e.g., by the Ottoman Empire. In Africa, powerful tribes conquered and enslaved members of weaker tribes—and, based on such an indigenous practice, tribal chiefs often found it lucrative to sell victims first to Islamic slave drivers and later to Europeans.

Even the British and Americans practiced the odious institution well into the 19th century until their germinating principle of individual rights extinguished it. In the 19th century, the British conducted a world-wide crusade against slavery and succeeded to a significant degree in stamping it out—but not in the Arab-Islamic world. Today, Sudan and Mauritania are but two of the Islamic nations in which a minimum of hundreds of thousands of human beings are brutally enslaved.

Further, across extensive parts of the world, the entire female gender—*fully 50% of the human population*—is culturally and/or legally suppressed. The rights of women continue to be denied and violated *with full legal sanction* in many countries. In some Latin American countries, for example, the law only recognizes chaste women as potential rape victims; non-virgins are not under its protection. In Pakistan, the law effectively equates rape with adultery. Any sex outside of marriage is against the law. As a consequence, a raped woman, rather than the rapist(s), is often arrested and prosecuted. It is common for a rape victim, once in police custody, to be raped again—by the police. In Afghanistan, a mere ten years ago, the Taliban legally prohibited the education of girls—and women could be executed for non-compliance. Today, Taliban insurgents and their fanatical supporters continue to assassinate women courageous enough to seek an independent life.

In Saudi Arabia, nobody is certain how many impoverished Asian and African women are lured to domestic jobs—and then forced to labor under slavery-like conditions. They can be beaten, starved, and sexually abused with no recourse to legal defense. Females are so right-less that in 2002 the religious police in Mecca hindered firefighters in their effort to rescue teenage girls from a burning school. As a result fifteen girls perished; they were not covered from head to foot and consequently unfit to be touched or even seen by male firefighters.

In China, traditional culture strongly favors boys over girls and most families prefer a son. Add to this situation the Communist government's imposition of a one-child-per-family policy—and the result is a prescription for catastrophe. Tens of thousands of infant girls are abandoned annually. Some are murdered, many are left to molder and die on heaps of refuse.

In numerous African countries the ghastly practice of female genital mutilation is routinely imposed. Generally without the victim's consent, she has her clitoris surgically removed so as to minimize her experience of pleasure during sexual intercourse. As if such coercive mutilation were not sufficiently barbaric, the procedure is often performed by medically inept amateurs, leading to extensive health problems and even death for the victims.

Today, in 2010, iron-fisted dictatorships in North Korea, Cuba, Myanmar, Iran, and Syria, as well as in Sudan and elsewhere, enslave and murder large portions of their indigenous populations and/or sponsor terrorist assaults against innocent civilians and freer nations. North Korea, in particular, considered the most repressive dictatorship on earth, is a slave state; hundreds of thousands of political prisoners toil as slave laborers in the country's gulags and stunted, half-starved civilians cower in their darkened hovels at night when a country-wide curfew is imposed and all electricity is extinguished, if it has not previously failed.

Examples of such inhuman barbarities can be recounted until innocent men recoil from the incessant horror. But most shocking is that so few honest persons ever raise the question: What is the fundamental cause of these atrocities? If they asked the question in this form and context, they would discover that the cause is statism—the cause is collectivism—the cause is the belief that only groups, and not an individual, are important—the cause is the widely held and tragically mistaken principle that an individual's life belongs not to him but to the tribe, the society, the nation, the group, the collective.

The cause is the utter repudiation of the principle of inalienable individual rights.

Across vast portions of the globe, the government retains the legal power to initiate force against innocent men. It is as if we, the human race, despite significant intellectual advances in the arts, science, and technology, have not made similar advances in morality and persist in the primitive practices of prehistoric savages.

The concept of individual rights is a revolutionary moral principle. Its birth awaited the 18th century Enlightenment—so that for millions of years, and throughout endless tribal warfare, men subsisted without it; and even then, its (partial) understanding and implementation was limited largely to Britain and America. It briefly gained currency in the West—and scarcely there—where it clung to a precarious intellectual existence, locked in a death struggle with countless species of statism. In its infancy, it clashed with feudalism and monarchy; in its maturity, with every form of socialism—be it Communism, National Socialism, or mixed economy welfare statism. Even Britain and America neither fully understood nor consistently practiced the principle, violating it repeatedly in the form of slavery, and/or imperialism, and/or mixed economy semi-socialism. But they originated a moral revolution.

The Caribbean researcher on the nature and history of slavery, Orlando Patterson, concludes that "there was no word for freedom in most non-Western languages before contact with Western peoples." In the absence of any understanding of individual rights, there could not be.

Today, even in the Western world, the principle of individual rights is dismissed, and is rarely even mentioned, much less seriously discussed. Intellectuals and moralists speak at times of "human rights" or, sometimes, of "civil rights," but never of "individual rights." But, in truth, there are no rights in the absence of individual rights. So-called "human rights" or "civil rights" are collectivist concepts that focus men's attention on groups. Such terms are fomented and deployed by socialists and welfare statists. In accordance with the principles they employ—and the one they deny, evade or ignore—they decry atrocities perpetrated on large groups while advocating the pillaging of a successful individual in order to re-distribute his wealth to those unsuccessful.

Advocates of "human rights" and/or "civil rights" rely implicitly on individual rights. Honest men, especially in America, recognize that an individual has a right to his own life, even if this principle is held as a hazy, half-formed, unarticulated idea. It is such a recognition that enables men to identify injustice against innocent individuals—and that provides the moral conviction to redress such injustices.

Observe in this regard that any successful attempt to protect innocent men from brutes—e.g., the ending of coercive racial segregation in the American South—rests logically upon the principle of individual rights. Why, for example, was it immoral to legally prevent a black man or woman from buying a home in a white neighborhood? Only because an individual human being—regardless of race or ethnicity—has the right to buy a home from whoever is voluntarily willing to sell to him. (And it was, similarly, the right of the white owner to sell to whomever he chose among those voluntarily willing and able to buy.) Why was it immoral, indeed, criminally brutal to assault or rape or lynch an innocent man or woman? Given the principle of individual rights—*and only given this principle*—the answer is manifest.

Notice also the tragic failure to successfully apply the principle of "human rights" in North Korea or Sudan or Myanmar or Rwanda, etc., countries and cultures that have, as yet, developed no understanding of or commitment to a principle of inalienable individual rights. Strictly speaking, there is no "human rights" movement (and no "civil rights" movement). There is and can be only an "individual rights" movement.

As Ayn Rand pointed out: the individual is the smallest minority on earth—and the one most relentlessly persecuted.

Where any and all understanding, support for, and protection of individual rights is unknown, there exists no moral principle to constrain the state (or the tribe or the race or the collective, et. al.) from disposing of an individual's life as it dictates. On collectivist premises, the state may plunder, enslave or murder a man (or any subset of them) at its will. Such a harsh truth explains why it is both appalling and heartbreaking—but not shocking—that today, 225 years after the American Revolution freedom is still virtually unknown throughout large portions of the world.

The principle of individual rights represents a moral revolution tragically unknown throughout much of the world and most of its history.

Statism and collectivism have been the historic status quo, and remain so in the 21st century. This means that the government's legal initiation of force against innocent men and women has been and remains the status quo. It is grimly inevitable, therefore, that tyranny, slavery, and mass murder have been the historic status quo—and remain so.

The principle of individual rights was culturally and politically prominent only in the Western world and only during the 18th and 19th centuries. Consequently, political-economic freedom was born there and then, monarchies were overthrown, tyrannies were toppled, serfdom was expunged, abolitionism was originated, and slavery was extinguished. Even the principle's faint legacy in the 20th century West was sufficient to conceive movements protecting the rights of ethnic minorities and women—movements that do not and cannot exist in those extensive portions of the globe that have never, even minimally, recognized a principle of individual rights.

What might a world achieve in which individual rights is fully understood and implemented—and where this principle need struggle no longer against multiple forms of its antithesis? What might a world achieve that institutes a universal ban on the initiation of force—thereby establishing the minimal conditions of civilized society—and proceeds to protect the moral and legal right of every individual to develop his/her mind and actualize his/her life?

Marx and Engels infamously opened *The Communist Manifesto* with the ominous line: "A specter is haunting Europe—the specter of communism." They were mistaken. The truth is vastly worse. A monster is trampling the globe—the monster of collectivism.

How many more human holocausts must be perpetrated before men gag on the blood of their brothers and sisters and resolve, finally, to call their permanent halt?

It is time to do so.

Indeed, it is long past time that civilized men who claim to venerate human life discover the moral principle without which human life cannot be preserved. It is long past time that civilized men took principled action to redress such a ghastly state of affairs. This small book represents an attempt to do precisely that—to warn rational men about the ongoing moral catastrophe, to identify its underlying causation, and, above all, to point to the sole means of resolution, and to do so now, while civilization clings to life and there is yet time.

PART ONE

THE HISTORIC SUPERIORITY OF CAPITALISM

Chapter One

The Dismal Poverty of the Pre-Capitalist Political-Economic Systems

In modern Western society we often take for granted the achievements of capitalism. The industrialization, the inventiveness, the technological progress so characteristic of the capitalist system is all around us. We drive to work or school in our cars, flood our homes with electric light, warm them against winter's cold with gas, oil or electric heat, cool them during summer's hot months with air conditioning, write on the personal computer, shop on the Internet, fly comfortably to distant destinations on jets, cleanse clothes and dishes in washing machines, cure diseases by means of antibiotics—and, above all, live in a country whose refrigerators and supermarkets are stocked with an overflowing abundance of life-giving food.

As a result, the life expectancy nears eighty years—and continues to rise.

But what of the societies that have not implemented capitalism—what are they like? What are the living conditions there? Do the non-capitalist political-economic systems enjoy the same living standards or life expectancies? Individual rights is a moral principle central to the preservation of human life. But what are its practical consequences? Specifically, what are the economic results of its implementation? And the practical results where and when it is unknown?

The first place to look in answer is to the conditions that existed immediately prior to the capitalist revolution of the late 18th century.

Many writers and historians speak glowingly of a "lost Golden Age" prior to the development of capitalism, industrialization, and the factory system, in which workers lived happily in freedom and prosperity. Friedrich Engels, the Communist writer and collaborator of Karl Marx, is representative of this school of thought.

Of the pre-industrial workers he says that "their standard of life was much better than that of the factory workers today [1840s.] They were not forced to work excessive hours; they themselves fixed the length of the working day and still earned enough for their needs." They had time for recreation, and played "bowls and football" with their neighbors. If children helped their parents work, it "was only an occasional employment and there was no question of an eight-or twelve-hour day." In the absence of extensive child labor, "workers' children were brought up at home...Children grew up in idyllic simplicity and in happy intimacy with their playmates."

The anti-capitalist writers do not stop there. They go on to claim that the factory system developed by industrial capitalists of the late 18th and early 19th centuries lowered the workers' living standards, causing widespread poverty and misery. The influential British historians, J.L. and Barbara Hammond, writing of English life claimed that the Industrial Revolution "fell like a war or a plague" on the workers. It allegedly crammed men, women, and children into the mills under unsanitary conditions, and forced them into long hours of inhuman toil in exchange for pitiably low wages. "Surely never since the days when populations were sold into slavery did a fate more sweeping overtake a people than the fate that covered the hills and valleys of Lancashire and the West Riding with the factory towns..."

The critics of capitalism arrived at two general conclusions regarding its early days: the first that the workers' living conditions were generally satisfactory (or at least bearable) in the pre-capitalist era—and the second that the factory system of the capitalists lowered those living standards significantly, if not drastically. The truth, however, is that both claims are profoundly, egregiously false. The truth is that capitalism raised worker's living standards to heights undreamed of prior to its inception—and began such a process of economic advance from its earliest days.

THE ABYSMAL DESTITUTION OF PRE-CAPITALIST EUROPE

Prior to the advent of industrial capitalism in Great Britain in the late 18th century, the lot of the English working class was an impoverished misery beyond anything witnessed in the modern Western world for centuries.

Famine—death for countless thousands by starvation—was widespread. Sanitation and sewerage were non-existent—filth, excrement, and vermin filled the streets of city and town and the ramshackle hovels of the poor; consequently, lethal disease of every variety imaginable, including the dreaded bubonic plague—the infamous "Black Death"—was inescapable, especially among the numberless poor. To say that incomes were depressed would be a gross understatement—by the standards of the coming capitalist era they were off-the-charts low. The grim result? On the eve of the Industrial Revolution in the mid-18th century, life expectancy in Great Britain was under 35 years.

To men of the modern industrial West, the rampant, horrific destitution of pre-capitalist Europe is inconceivable. For example, according to eminent

French historian, Fernand Braudel, by a test employed in Lyons, France in the 17th century, the poverty level was reached only when a man's daily income was insufficient to buy him a crust of bread. *The heartbreaking truth is that a quarter to half the population of 17th century England subsisted chronically near, at or below this level of penury.*

To put this in perspective, consider the following: if the U.S. Bureau of Labor were to today employ a similar standard of poverty, Americans considered below the poverty line would be limited to those making no more than $18.00 per month—or $216.00 per year. (So somebody making $19.00 per month--$228.00 per year—would generate an income too high to be considered poor.)

According to Angus Maddison, a leading economic historian, Europe suffered through *zero economic growth* in the centuries from 500AD to 1500—and per capita income stood at an abysmally low $215.00 in 1500. European economic growth was at the paltry rate of 0.1 percent in the centuries from 1500 to 1700 and per capita income was an estimated $265.00 at the turn of the 18th century.

Historians differ regarding its extent but they agree that death by famine was prevalent in Europe in the centuries prior to the Industrial Revolution, including in Britain. One researcher, Andrew Appleby, wrote: "In 1587-88, 1597 and 1623, the northwestern English counties of Cumberland and Westmoreland were struck by famine. In those years, thousands of people starved..." It is likely that with edible food unobtainable, the poor ate the bark from trees and "unripe grain, roots, grass, and the intestines and blood of animals that had been slaughtered as food for the better-off." Fatality from starvation must be understood broadly enough to include death from intestinal disorders induced by eating such unsuitable foods, as well as "pure" starvation, in which "caloric intake is reduced to the point where bodily functions slowly cease..."

It is certainly possible that starvation among the English poor was too common to elicit any comment—but conditions were even worse in other parts of Europe. Again from Braudel: A 1662 French report stated: "Famine this year has put an end to over ten thousand families...and forced a third of the inhabitants...to eat wild plants." Another commentator said: "Some people ate human flesh." Even accounting for exaggeration, the situation was dire. In the same era, another French writer claimed: "The people of Lorraine...are reduced to such extremities that, like animals, they eat the grass in the meadows...and are as black and thin as skeletons."

A leading 20th century Italian historian, Carlo Cipolla, corroborated this assessment: "It is difficult for those living in the industrialized countries of the 20th century to imagine hunger and famine. People literally died of hunger, and it was not unusual to find men dead at the roadside, their mouths full of grass and their teeth sunk in the earth."

In Germany, "famine was a persistent visitor to the towns and the flatlands." In Scotland, the so-called "Lean Years" of 1697-1703 saw widespread crop failure and harrowing suffering. "No one knows how many died during the famine...but they probably numbered in the tens of thousands"—a significant number of persons in a country of fewer than two million inhabitants. In the same period, a horrific tragedy struck Finland. Braudel states: "If one wants to measure the catastrophes of history by the proportion of victims claimed, the 1696-97 famine in Finland *must be regarded as the most terrible event in European history.* A quarter or a third of the Finnish population disappeared at that time." (Emphasis added.)

In succinctly summing up such horrors, Braudel concluded: "Famine occurred so insistently for centuries on end that it became incorporated into man's biological regime and built into his daily life. Dearth and penury were continual and familiar, even in Europe...famine only disappeared from the West at the close of the eighteenth century, or even later."

SANITATION, SEWAGE, AND DISEASE

One of the extraordinary achievements of modern technology—and one utterly taken for granted—is the availability of clean drinking water to hundreds of millions of persons. For such an accomplishment to be reached, reservoirs must be built, steel must be perfected and plentifully manufactured, and vast networks of sealed, separate, and unleaking water mains and sewerage pipes must be constructed across an entire continent. Then and only then, can individuals enjoy the life-giving advantages of clean drinking water and indoor plumbing.

Such advances were not attained until the turn of the 20th century—and even then only in the Western capitalist nations.

The main health problem confronting any non-industrialized society is: how to keep human and animal waste products out of the drinking water. The grim answer is: it cannot be done. Waste products inevitably seep into the ground water or, worse, get dumped directly into rivers and streams, thereby tainting the drinking water. The result is widespread and early death from such diseases as cholera, typhoid, and chronic dysentery—maladies largely wrought by the drinking of impure water. In the absence of advanced technology and industrialization, there is no effective means of purifying the water. As with recurrent famine, such diseases too were the lot of the masses in pre-capitalist Europe.

Such British historians as Mabel Buer, M. Dorothy George, and J.J. Bagley report that in London, as late as the 19th century so much sewage was still dumped into the Thames that "the windows of the Houses of Parliament could never be opened because of the stench..." For centuries leading into the modern era sanitation was virtually non-existent. "Street cleaning defeated the authorities of every medieval town...house-holders persisted in dumping refuse and sewage in the streets, and allowing their animals and poultry to foul public thoroughfares at will. Few people concerned themselves if dead animals lay about unburied for days...The channel which ran down the middle of most streets became an open sewer..." Drinking water often came from such streams as the Walbrook, the Fleet, and the River Thames, "the ultimate destination of most of London's garbage and sewage."

A terrible consequence is that the absence of effective sanitation and sewage meant the proliferation of vermin and germs. The fleas carried by rats caused the bubonic plague—a ghastly horror that afflicted Europe for centuries. In the years of 1347-1350 the gruesome "Black Death" swept the European continent, including Britain, *snuffing out an estimated 25 million human lives, roughly one-third of Western Europe's total population.* Nor was this an isolated occurrence. In the 16th century alone, the plague struck in 1509, 1514, 1526, 1560, and 1576. In the 1720s, it ravaged Marseilles. In Italy, the famous Church of Santa Maria della Salute in Venice was built as a shrine to the Virgin Mary in gratitude for relief from a plague that killed 47,000 in that city alone between the years 1630-31. Indeed, Venice was struck by epidemics of plague twenty-one times between 1348 and 1630; Paris twenty-two times between 1348 and 1596; and Barcelona seventeen times between 1457 and 1590.

Nor was London spared such lethal outbreaks. Plague closed all London theaters between 1592 and 1594, providing the young, poor William Shakespeare the free time to write *Venus and Adonis* and *The Rape of Lucrece*, as well as to begin his celebrated sonnets. The 1593 epidemic killed approximately 18,000 in London, mostly in the rat-infested slums around the docks. Between 1348 and 1665, there were repeated outbreaks of plague; thirty epidemics between 1351 and 1485 alone, twelve of them on a nationwide scale. In the half-century concluding in 1593, England was afflicted with plague in greater than 50 percent of those years. A major epidemic in 1563 also killed roughly 18,000 in London, motivating a thirty-year-old Queen Elizabeth to decamp to Windsor, where she had constructed a gallows upon which to hang any resident of London sufficiently foolhardy to seek an audience.

Wretched Housing and Fire

The hovels of the poor in London and elsewhere were health hazards of the highest degree. Overcrowding was severe, and dirt, garbage, and filth ubiquitous. The houses were made of wood, not uncommonly rotting, and "infested with all kinds of vermin." Mabel Buer concluded: "From a health point of view the only thing to be said in their favor was that they burned down very easily."

Burn they did. On Sunday September 2, 1666, a fire started in the bakery of Thomas Farynor on Pudding Lane near the banks of the Thames. Biographer-historian Stephen Coote wrote: "Fires were a fact of life in London, a cheek-by-jowl infinity of timber-framed buildings ensured that this was so..." At first, the Lord Mayor responded contemptuously that "a woman could piss it out"—but it was tragically not to be. Filled with wooden houses and severely overcrowded conditions, and possessed of only primitive firefighting methods and equipment, London blazed unabated like the slums of Hell. When the Great Fire of London finally ran its course on Thursday September 6th, an area of one-and-a-half miles by one-half mile lay in ashes. Over 13,000 houses had been destroyed—and 100,000 persons faced a cold, homeless winter.

Only the previous year, London had suffered an outbreak of plague that had killed some 70,000 residents, almost 15% of the city's population. If there was any consolation regarding the 1666 disaster, it was that the Great Fire also destroyed large numbers of rats, fleas, and other vermin, possibly providing the city relief from further plague.

Britain was a "Third World" country prior to the Industrial Revolution—as was the rest of Europe. The rampant famine, the incessant outbreaks of plague and other lethal diseases, the encompassing, crushing poverty, the abysmally low life expectancy are akin to areas of Africa today, the world's poorest region.

But Third World Britain was vastly worse off than is Africa today. For at least in contemporary Africa—for all of its unrestrained tribalism, dictatorship, and internecine warfare—there is some benefit from modern agriculture, electricity, automobiles, airplanes, antibiotics, even computers and the Internet, etc. As a consequence, life expectancies in many African nations are significantly higher than the under-35 years of Third World Britain—with many in the 50s. (Although areas of contemporary Africa are very similar to pre-industrialized Third World Europe, including a life expectancy in the 30s.) The above advances were not available in pre-industrial Britain for the simple reason that none had yet been invented. They are all a product of the subsequent era of industrial capitalism.

Even acknowledging the extreme difficulty in identifying the living standards of past centuries to any degree of precision, it is clear that by the standards of modern capitalism, they were tragically low. From pure humaneness it is incumbent to identify the causes of such anguish—to ensure non-recurrence in the nations that subsequently overcame it, and to promote eradication in the extensive portions of the globe where it yet proliferates. The causes are economic but in larger part philosophic.

THE ECONOMIC CAUSES OF WIDESPREAD POVERTY

Prior to the Technological and Industrial Revolutions consumer goods were made by hand—by the effort of men's arms and backs, by the force of animals' bodies in addition, by muscle power. *By such paltry means alone it is impossible to produce vast quantities of goods.* Put simply: limited to such primitive methods of production, men cannot create a supply of goods sufficient to raise living standards above bare subsistence for millions of human beings.

The fundamental principle of economics is the Law of Supply and Demand. If supply of a good is low relative to the demand for it, the price will increase. On the other hand, if the supply of a good is high relative to demand, its price will decline. The only means to ensure prices sufficiently low to be affordable by millions is to produce a vastly increased supply of the good in demand. This cannot be done by mere manual labor and muscle power.

In the absence of advanced science, technology, and industry, for example, men lack both knowledge of agricultural science and ability to create agricultural machinery. They will not know how to rotate crops, how to protect livestock from disease and crops from blight or insect swarm, and they will lack tractors, combines, and other mechanized implements of farm technology. Helpless against insect infestation and disease—at the mercy of storm, drought, and bitter cold—reduced to hand plows pulled by mule or ox—it was tragically inevitable that food production was meager and lethal famine rampant.

Thomas Malthus was definitively correct, although in a limited sense and context: *in a non-capitalist society, population growth will inescapably outstrip food supply.*

What is true of food is equally true of every necessity of human survival. Prior to the Industrial Revolution and the factory system, clothing, for example, was produced on hand looms. The manufacture of a single shirt (or any other article of clothing) took a great deal of time and effort; the supply of shirts, consequently, was low—and prices correspondingly high, too high for the overwhelming preponderance of the population. The result was that most persons owned a single set of clothes, often best described as "rags," and wore it continuously.

Because regular bathing contributes to wear and tear, these clothes were generally unwashed for months on end. The hygienic and medical problems resulting from infestations of lice and other vermin were severe. In the absence of industrialization and factories, and, above all, without James Watts' steam engine to drive the power looms, it was impossible to manufacture the vast supply of clothing necessary to attain affordable prices for millions.

This principle applies just as fully to the construction of shelter. Imagine the difference, not just in back-breaking labor but in time, between constructing a home with merely shovels, pick axes, and hammers, on the one hand, or constructing it with steam shovels, derricks, cranes, and electrically powered tools on the other. High-powered tools drastically cuts the time required for the production of homes, thereby contributing to a vastly increased quantity of affordable housing. (Bear in mind that shovels, pick axes, and hammers must also be produced, so that in the absence of industrialization even their supply was severely limited.)

Further, prior to the Technological and Industrial Revolutions, men lacked the knowledge to mass produce steel—or even iron—and most building was necessarily done with wood. This made impossible the erection of apartment buildings (or any high-rise construction), thereby severely diminishing the housing available to most members of society. Such facts make it clear that and why home ownership for millions became a reality only during the capitalist, industrial era, prior to which there existed not the slightest possibility of it.

Such advances in technology and industrialization are necessary to mass produce and consequently lower the price of any and all commodities, including those indispensable to human life. In the absence of mass production of the necessities of survival, mass numbers of human beings will not survive— or will survive for minimal duration with maximal tribulation.

But why did the Technological and Industrial Revolutions await the capitalist revolution of 18th century Britain? Given the desperate need—worldwide and centuries-old—of such advances, why then and why there? For answers, we need to look beyond the boundaries of economics to the field of philosophy.

THE PHILOSOPHIC CAUSES OF WIDESPREAD POVERTY

Advances in applied science, technology, and industrialization depend upon advances in theoretical science. In effect, the achievements of such inventors and entrepreneurs as James Watt, Thomas Edison, the Wright brothers, Andrew Carnegie, et. al., are built on foundations laid by such scientists as Isaac Newton and others.

Such inventors, entrepreneurs, innovators, and scientists are geniuses.

Contrary to Marx, Engels, and an entire school of socialist intellectuals, the fundamental cause of economic progress is not manual labor. It is, as Ayn Rand brilliantly dramatizes in *Atlas Shrugged*, mind power. Manual labor is undoubtedly required for construction of all kinds and its productive application represents an unmitigated virtue. Further, innovative thinkers (Edison, for example) might perform a fair amount of it as part of their innovations. But they are not glorified tinkerers. They are intellectual giants.

The first cause and prime mover of scientific, technological, and industrial progress is human genius. James Watt, for example, spent years studying the properties of steam with leading scientists at the University of Glasgow. Thomas Edison devoured every book he could purchase on electrical engineering. The Wright brothers did the same regarding aeronautical engineering. It was their minds that such thinkers developed.

It is eminently logical, therefore, that where man's mind is free, progress in all intellectual fields is maximized—and where it is repressed, such advances are aborted.

Which social conditions are necessary for the full flowering of human intellect? What type of political-economic system promotes the development of the independent reasoning mind? And which type(s) retard, restrict, and/ or outright prohibit its free functioning? Let us answer the latter question immediately.

A curious person need not look far for the causes of the mind's suppression in pre-capitalist Europe. The culprit was: feudalism and its political legacy; the *ancien regime*—the reign of the monarchy, the lesser aristocracy, and the official, established, unchallengeable state religion.

The glorification and unquestioned authority of the aristocracy severely denigrated the worth of so-called commoners, i.e., the common man, necessitating that the overwhelming preponderance of human minds went unvalued, undeveloped, and unused. For example, how many potential Isaac Newtons, Thomas Jeffersons, Benjamin Franklins, James Watts, Thomas Edisons, Andrew Carnegies, et. al., were compelled to live in utter bondage, slaving away as manual laborers in the fields of the nobility—or, at the very least, threatened with imprisonment, torture, even execution if their radical ideas clashed with the precepts of king, aristocracy, or clergy?

Illustrations of legalized repression abound: Denis Diderot, the French writer and prime mover behind mankind's first encyclopedia, a gigantic undertaking in support of widespread human knowledge, was incarcerated for his ideas. Voltaire admired Britain as a mecca of intellectual freedom, wrote brilliantly and scathingly against the oppression of French king, aristocracy, and clerics—and, in consequence, found himself repeatedly imprisoned and exiled for thoughts offensive to suppressive authority. D'Alembert, the scientist and writer, was intimidated into temporarily severing his connection with the *Encyclopedie*. Galileo was threatened with torture and Giordano Bruno burned at the stake because their thinking clashed with that of the Inquisition.

(In tragic irony, the French Revolution, in the name of liberty established a crushing dictatorship briefly as lethal as that which for a millennium preceded it; imprisoning, for example, the philosopher, Condorcet, who died mysteriously, and beheading the scientist, Lavoisier, *the father of modern chemistry*. Repression, may it come under sundry names and guises, has but one obdurate reality: the stifling of free inquiry.)

Further, such infamous events occurred in the 17th and 18th centuries, in the post-Renaissance period when commitment to the independent reasoning mind was growing. The suppression had been far more comprehensive in earlier centuries when "heretics"— i.e., independent thinkers who possessed the temerity to challenge official religious orthodoxy, and who included such serious intellectual challengers as the Arians, the Pelagians, and the Manicheans—were often burned at the stake (or put to the sword) by the thousands. To ensure the death of their ideas in conjunction with their bodies, their books were often burned.

The creative mind cannot function under such a reign of terror. Its holy quest for knowledge does not permit it to cease asking challenging questions, to second-guess truthful principles, to gaze over its shoulder for the Inquisition's haunting presence, or to impose self-censorship because compelled to live in chronic dread of its freedom, even its life.

If an individual's life belongs to the king or Church, then so does his mind, which is legally permitted to "think" only within the framework of ideas deemed palatable by the authorities. If such are the social parameters imposed, then rational inquiry is curtailed, even stifled; the fundamental cause of human advance is abrogated, and many men will not survive in the ages of miserable ignorance and penury that necessarily ensue.

But the intellectual forces supporting the mind, science, and freedom against unquestioning obedience to the ancient regime had been gathering momentum since the Renaissance. The men of the 18th century had witnessed the historical evidence: after all, Michelangelo had not been an aristocrat, nor had Leonardo. Nor were Galileo, Shakespeare, Descartes, Milton, Locke, Newton or numerous other geniuses. Such facts supporting the efficacy and potential stature of the common man could not be overlooked. The leading thinkers of the 18th century Enlightenment, building on their inheritance from the Renaissance and the Age of Reason, recognized the latent power and validity of everyman's mind and succeeded in sweeping away centuries of aristocratic and clerical prejudices, eventually unleashing countless millions to employ their minds, seek an education, think, innovate, and advance.

The battle for the freedom of man's mind had been a centuries-long death struggle. Finally, in the 18th century men stood at the threshold of triumph. Finally, during the Enlightenment and of its essence, liberated human brain power would bring relief from centuries of pervasive suffering.

Chapter Two
The Heroes of Capitalism

The starvation-level living standards, the encompassing misery, the appallingly-low life expectancies described in the previous chapter are unknown in the industrialized, capitalist nations today. Why? Because of the great men about to be discussed. These heroes, operating under conditions of increasing political-economic liberty in Great Britain and America, wrought unprecedented advances in applied science, engineering, inventiveness, and industrialization, thereby transfiguring the modern world.

Our story begins in 18th century Scotland, the cradle of modern industrial civilization. Scotland was the poorest country of Europe—but it was on the verge of becoming the most accomplished nation in the world.

For although very few people today remember it, *the Scottish Enlightenment was the first cause and prime mover of the British Industrial Revolution*. As stated by Voltaire: "It is to Scotland that we look for our ideas of civilization."

A leading intellectual light of 18th century Scotland was James Watt (1736-1819), the representative inventor of the age. Watt perfected Thomas Newcomen's steam engine, thereby creating "the work engine of the Industrial Revolution." He grew up surrounded by the paraphernalia of seagoing Glasgow, a largely self-taught man. He was instrument maker for the University of Glasgow, where he amazed the professors with his knowledge and mental prowess. "I saw a workman, and expected no more, but was surprised to find a philosopher," said John Robison, later professor of natural philosophy at the University of Edinburgh and a leading contributor to the *Encyclopedia Britannica*, the era's most comprehensive compendium of state-of-the-art knowledge.

Watt was no mere paragon of mechanical tinkering; he was a careful student of the properties and power of steam. He was friend, assistant, and pupil to one of the period's leading scientists, Joseph Black, professor of chemistry, medicine, and anatomy at the University of Glasgow. Black, who isolated and gave a detailed account of carbon dioxide, discovered the principle of latent heat in 1761 and three years later measured its quantity in steam. Watt, Black, Robison, and other university thinkers had been examining the properties of steam for years when, on a walk early in 1765, Watt hit on the idea of separate condensation, which permitted his engine to generate a constant motion.

"Nature has its weak side," Watt said, "if only we can find it." That, of course, was the task of science—one manfully undertaken at the 18th century Scottish universities.

During this period the leading English schools were still dominated by religious prejudice and authoritarian dogma. For one thing, Oxford, Cambridge, and other English centers of learning were open only to members of the Church of England. Dissenters—non-believers in the official state religion—were not admitted. Nor was such irrational bias limited to their admission standards; their cognitive method was largely uncritical acceptance of the teachings of ancient and medieval authorities, rather than rational examination of observational facts

But the Scottish universities at Glasgow and Edinburgh were open to Dissenters, the most active thinkers among whom flocked there. Many of Great Britain's best minds—those most conscientious in observing data and vigorous in pursuit of critical inquiry taught and studied there, including at the superlative University of Edinburgh medical school.

Philosophically, reason is a method that begins with, and is undeviatingly devoted to, the factual information provided by sense perception. It then proceeds in accordance with the principles of logic to formulate theories that consistently explain—and neither contradict nor explain away—such sensory information. Historically, such a method was created by the Greeks, perfected by Aristotle (who, for all of his errors, made enormous advances in biology, as well as in logic and philosophy), and was responsible for the great achievements of the Classical world.

The medievals replaced it with faith and blind obedience to authority, an intellectual method dominant for 1000 years and largely responsible for the infamous Dark Age of the 5th to the 9th centuries. Many great Classical works—preeminently Aristotle's writings—were lost during this period; were re-discovered in Islamic Spain; and re-introduced to the West, largely by such great Aristotelian thinkers as Albertus Magnus and Thomas Aquinas.

Centuries later, the great thinkers of the Renaissance and the Age of Reason shattered the Western mind's cognitive dependence on authorities (one leading example of whom in this era was, sadly and ironically, Aristotle) and returned it to the Greek mindset of studying nature, not the supernatural, and by employment of observation-based rationality, not by means of faith in a revealed text and/or uncritical reliance on established authorities.

The great English philosopher, John Locke (1632-1704), played an important role in this re-assessment and re-establishment of a proper reasoning method. In his influential book, *An Essay Concerning Human Understanding*, Locke argued that all human knowledge, regardless of complexity or technicality, originated ultimately in ordinary sense experience, and not in innate ideas (i.e., knowledge implanted in the human mind from birth) or divine revelation. That being the case, the knowledge required for right living took no specialized expertise, no cultivated capacity to interpret Holy Scripture or explicate principles deeply embedded in the human mind. It took rather observation of nature and the application of rational intelligence, which were capacities possessed by every individual, regardless of religion, birth, or social class.

In practice, the exemplar of this monumental change in the way men sought knowledge was Isaac Newton (1642-1727), the greatest scientist of history. The specific identifications and advances discovered by this great man were revolutionary; even more so was his cognitive method—his means of employing his mind—and the influence it exerted on the thinkers of the 18th century.

Philosopher, Ernst Cassirer, describes Newton's method: "The procedure is thus not from concepts and axioms to phenomena, but vice-versa. Observation produces the datum of science; the principle and law are the object of the investigation."

Put simply: learning proceeds from the facts of observation to the laws of nature that explain those facts—and not vice-versa; not from an interpreting of facts in accordance with pre-conceived ideas, content-less theories formed prior to experience, or irrational prejudices. Such a misconceived method results, metaphorically speaking, in the forcing of square pegs into round holes—or, perhaps more precisely, in a futile attempt to snugly wrap an object bristling with square pegs in a blanket designed with exclusively round holes.

The University of Edinburgh medical school pre-eminently implemented this new scientific methodology of the age: it emphasized a Newtonian observation-based rationality—a reverence for facts, objective knowledge, and critical thought in contrast to the authoritarian dogmas of the past. Such a reason-oriented, unprejudicial outlook and spirit contributed to the religious freedom of the Scottish universities and helped attract to them many of Great Britain's most brilliant minds. Without this realization, it will be inexplicable—as opposed to merely astonishing—how many outstanding engineers and scientists (not merely physicians) studied medicine at the University of Edinburgh in the subsequent century, a list that includes Charles Darwin.

The University of Edinburgh, especially its medical school, became a fountainhead of the Scottish Enlightenment, including its Industrial Revolution, because of its superlative emphasis on the new cognitive method of Newtonian science.

The leading Scottish universities were the conduit transmitting the Enlightenment method of observation-based rationality to the best minds across Great Britain, including in England, a select number of whom centered in

Birmingham, where James Watt moved to perfect and manufacture his steam engine.

THE LUNAR SOCIETY OF BIRMINGHAM

In the 18th century's second half, at the Enlightenment's zenith, a diverse array of scientific, technological, and manufacturing talent gathered in the area of Birmingham, England, that is perhaps matchless in the history of industry.

Watt, in his new partnership with Matthew Boulton, owner of the Soho Engineering Works, found a mind that was brilliantly able regarding issues of engineering and applied science. Further, Boulton, already well-established in business, employed the artisans Watt required to create the engine's fragile mechanisms.

Speaking to James Boswell, famed biographer of Samuel Johnson, Boulton proclaimed proudly in 1776: "I sell here, sir, what all the world desires to have — Power."

Boulton's splendid words could and should be the exultant motto of industrial capitalism. For there is power to create and power to destroy — power over nature and power over men — power to do good and power to do evil. The Watt and Boulton steam engine pioneered the mass production of consumer goods, the capacity to manufacture the enormous quantity of commodities necessary to the prosperity, indeed the literal survival of millions of human beings. Such ability to bring flourishing life where previously had existed mass squalor and unrelieved suffering represents a good of historically unprecedented proportions, abundantly justifying the ringing grandeur of Matthew Boulton's pithy statement.

Watt and Boulton were integral members of an extraordinary group of physicians-scientists-inventors-entrepreneurs that met regularly to further the related causes of research, technology, industry, and manufacturing.

The Lunar Society of Birmingham, so-called because it convened at the time of the full moon when its light most brilliantly illuminated the still primitive roads, was at its zenith during the late-1770s and 1780s. Its list of members reads like a "Who's Who" of 18th century British scientific, technological, and industrial talent.

In addition to Watt and Boulton, the group included Erasmus Darwin, one of England's most able physicians (Edinburgh trained), an inventor, botanist, poet, all-around original mind, and grandfather of Charles Darwin. Another superb physician, William Withering, was a member, an outstanding researcher who introduced the use of digitalis into medical practice, constituting a revolution in the history of cardiac care. Withering, also Edinburgh-trained, later became noted for his botanical studies, as did his great rival, Darwin.

Josiah Wedgewood, the innovative producer of pottery and founder of the company that centuries later still bears his name, could not be overlooked in any group, however exalted. Based on extensive experimentation, Wedgewood created earthenware pottery for common use that was of comparable quality to the expensive service he produced for royalty. In time, his advances transformed the kitchens of the working class and made Wedgewood a wealthy man. Additionally, he designed an innovative method of measuring a kiln's high temperatures, thereby pioneering new techniques used to resolve that ancient and intractable difficulty. He was, it should be noted, Charles Darwin's other grandfather.

The chemist, James Keir, made significant contributions to the group. He also studied medicine at Edinburgh — and was nephew to James Lind, the Edinburgh-trained physician who discovered a cure for scurvy. Keir translated an advanced French Dictionary of Chemistry, served as a science consultant to Boulton, opened the Tipton Chemical Works — a chemical plant equal in size to any in England — and produced a new metallic alloy jointly developed by he and Boulton. .

Not to go unmentioned in this circle of extraordinary men was William Small, who studied medicine at the University of Glasgow. Small became professor of natural philosophy and mathematics at William and Mary College in Virginia, where his teachings so inspired the young Thomas Jefferson, who was his daily companion, that the future President of the United States remarked that Small's influence "fixed the destinies of my life." Small introduced the lecture method in Virginia, contributed to the subsequent science curricula of the United States, was a friend of Benjamin Franklin, took out several patents for the improvement of clocks, and was physician to Boulton and science advisor to Watt.

But it was when Joseph Priestley moved to Birmingham in 1780 that the Lunar Society reached its apogee. Priestley, chemist par excellence, Unitarian minister, friend of Franklin, and radical free thinker, was one of the great scientists of his or any age. It was Priestley who isolated and described several gases, including oxygen, as well as ammonia, nitrous oxide, sulfur dioxide, and carbon monoxide. Encouraged by Franklin, who he met in London in 1766, Priestley conducted experiments in the new field of electricity, and wrote his *History of Electricity* the following year.

During his decade in Birmingham, Priestley served as science advisor to Wedgewood, as he had for years to his brother-in-law, "Iron Mad" John Wilkinson, who pioneered the use of cast iron, was among the first to produce iron boats and bridges, and whose foundry produced most of the machine parts for the firm of Boulton and Watt. In 1774 Wilkinson patented a process for boring cannon that he adapted to boring cylinders for Watt's engines with a new and matchless degree of accuracy. It was Wilkinson's new boring machine that finally made the steam engine feasible.

In the words of Robert Schofield, historian of the Lunar Society, Priestley was "no 'pure' scientist to be horrified by the suggestion that his work be turned to use...The mixing of science, applied science, and technology in Lunar activities found a supporter in Priestley" — and, "as an industrial research organization, [the Lunar Society] found in him also a paid consultant." The Lunar members provide a striking historical example of men who in Ayn

Rand's later terms desire to "live on earth." They sought to "make a practical use of scientific knowledge..." to create material advances, to thereby improve men's earthly lives, and "to make some discovery by which [a man] might increase his fortune."

Jenny Uglow, a more recent biographer of the group, observes that so many of the Lunar men were either Scots or educated at the University of Edinburgh—the cradle of the Scottish Enlightenment—"that at times it would seem as though Birmingham itself was an intellectual colony of Scotland."

The essence of the Scottish Enlightenment was not a pursuit of knowledge for its own sake. It cannot be sufficiently emphasized that its leading thinkers sought to advance knowledge for the emphatic purpose of practical application—to invent, innovate, and industrialize—to manufacture goods, grow food, cure disease—to raise men's living standards and to increase their life expectancies. A good example of this spirit was provided by the name of one of Scotland's elite intellectual circles—of which moral philosopher/economist, Adam Smith, was a key member: the Edinburgh Society for Encouraging Arts, Sciences, Manufactures and Agriculture in Scotland.

The Enlightenment's leading thinkers, often referred to as *philosophes*—from France to Scotland to England to Britain's North American colonies—were overwhelmingly concerned with a single interlocking set of principles: *to free human beings to pursue their own lives and thereby liberate independent minds to wreak life-giving practical advances.* What, for example, was the real world payoff of the Lunar Society's activities?

THE BIG BANG OF THE INDUSTRIAL REVOLUTION

A major part of the answer lies in the revolution wrought first in the clothing industry. The application of the Watt and Boulton steam engine to the manufacture of textiles in 1785 constituted the "Big Bang of the Industrial Revolution," adding enormous power to the already-increasing mechanization of the production of cotton clothing. First came such advances as the flying shuttle, the spinning jenny, the frame, and the "mule"—a cross-breed of the jenny and the frame; then came the stupendous power of the Watt and Boulton double-action rotative steam engine.

The practical results of such technological innovation were staggering. In 1765, for example, half a million pounds of cotton had been spun in England, all by hand. By 1784, 12 million pounds were spun, all by machine. In 1785 the powerful Watt and Boulton steam engines were first applied to spinning by rollers, and in the 1790s steam power was used to drive the mules. Production increased to the point that by 1812 the supply of cotton yarn was so enormous that its price had dropped to a mere 10 percent of what it had been previously.

Historian Paul Johnson makes the point succinctly: "By the early 1860s the price of cotton cloth...was less than 1 percent of what it had been in 1784, when the industry was already mechanized. There is no previous instance in world history of the price of a product in potentially universal demand coming down so fast." As a result, hundreds of millions of people worldwide were able to dress—at long last—comfortably, *cleanly, and hygienically.*

Nor were the technological advances of the era limited to the perfection and application of the steam engine. Britain's inventors, engineers, and industrialists wrought life-giving advances across a broad spectrum of related fields. Examples abound. "Iron Mad" John Wilkinson was but one prominent pioneer in the building revolution of the 18th century—by the 1790s he produced roughly one-eighth of Britain's cast iron. But Abraham Darby had previously discovered how to make iron by means of coke—not charcoal, which existed in diminishing supply—a process that greatly facilitated British production. British manufacture of iron jumped by a factor of ten between 1700 and 1800—from 25,000 to 250,000 tons. The enormous increase in available iron was necessary to erect bridges and factories, to build machines and the steam engine, to create more powerful and seaworthy ships—and, shortly to follow, to construct trains and rails.

Innovations build upon innovations, and significant advances in agriculture and food production were facilitated by invention of the Rotherham plow, which covered the moldboard with iron. (Subsequent to this, in 1837, the first steel plow, created by John Deere, proved so much more effective than earlier designs that it opened to agriculture regions of the United States previously deemed unsuited to it.) Technical improvements in agricultural implements were one reason that British wheat yield improved from 25 bushels per acre at the time of Waterloo to 47 bushels by the early 1850s.

Critical to living standards and life expectancies is sufficient food supply. The quantity and quality of food available to the common man during this era dramatically increased. For example, technological advances made possible "the development of deep-sea trawling;" when combined with improved transit facilitated by railroads, highways, and steamships, the result was an increased supply and consumption of fish. Further, because of growing commitment to individual rights, including that of free trade, onerous tariffs on imported grain—the notorious "Corn Laws"—were finally repealed, significantly expanding the country's bread supply. During the same era, and for the same reason, duties were reduced or even eliminated on meat, butter, cheese, and other foodstuffs. Economic historian, R. M. Hartwell, tells us: "The conclusion…is unquestionably that the amount and variety of food consumed increased between 1800 and 1850."

By the mid-19th century Britain was accurately referred to as "the workshop of the world," with world-leading industries in textiles, coal, iron and then steel, and railroading.

A related development necessary to spur industrial growth was the revolution in the transportation system. Road conditions in England were abysmal until almost the turn of the 19th century. They were generally little better than muddy ruts, often impassable. Historian, Arthur Herman, points out that conditions in Scotland were even worse. Roads in the Highlands barely existed, and local roads were so bad that in wet weather "horses sink to their bellies, and carts to their axles." This did not begin to change until the 1790s.

The engineer, John McAdam (1756-1836), devised a new method of road-building. Criss-crossing the breadth of Great Britain, traipsing some 30,000 miles, he inspected virtually every lane and back-woods path bestrewing the island. He used stone and crushed gravel to inexpensively improve roads, finding that the weight of wagon wheels and horses' hooves would "compact the layers of stone to form a hard surface"—a macadam surface.

Macadam roads were soon in service across Great Britain, immensely expediting land travel and transport. Travel time from London to Edinburgh, for example, was cut from ten days to two—and the journey from Glasgow to Edinburgh that formerly took Adam Smith a day-and-a-half was now done in four-and-a-half hours. The new method laid foundations for the subsequent innovation of binding road surfaces with tar—a surface known as tarmacadam or tarmac for short.

Another superlative Scottish engineer, Thomas Telford (1757-1834), created Britain's modern transportation system. His life story is an inspiring testament to the potentialities of the human spirit. His father, a shepherd in Glendenning, died shortly after his birth, and his widowed mother reared him in crushing poverty. He was literally born in a hovel consisting of four mud walls and a thatched roof. Through years of childhood labor necessary to attain minimal subsistence, he toiled further to master reading, writing, and mathematics.

His arduous exertion reaped dividends, for he subsequently made road-building into a science. He recognized the need of a level line of construction and built the London to Holyhead Road, now the A5, with its superlative suspension bridge spanning the Menai Straits. Scottish novelist, Walter Scott, called Menai Bridge: "the most impressive work of art he had ever seen."

But it was as a builder of canals that Telford reached his momentous achievements. In the years before the creation of railroads, water transport was the quickest and cheapest form of shipping heavy goods, including coal. He designed vast aqueducts for his Ellesmere Canal; Arthur Herman reports that one "rose 127 feet above the Dee River, on a one-hundred-foot raised bank...two hundred years later...it is still in use."

The Caledonian Canal, running through the Scottish Highlands, connected the Atlantic Ocean to the North Sea, presented seemingly insuperable engineering difficulties—consequently took Telford fifteen years to construct—but, upon completion, opened to trade for the first time the previously remote and wild areas of Scotland's north. Later, it served as the model for the Suez Canal.

The development of the railroad industry in Great Britain of the early 19th century followed the same pattern and continued the same themes. For one thing, the new mode of transport relied heavily on Watt's steam engine—that quintessential invention of the Scottish Enlightenment—and deployed brilliant scientific innovation in service of improved material conditions of man's earthly life.

Richard Trevithick, a Cornish blacksmith and wrestler—and an exceedingly inventive man—was an early creator of the locomotive. In the first years of the 19th century, he applied Watt's creation to the problem of locomotion and introduced a high-pressure engine capable of performing as a "mobile power pack." In London, in 1808, he demonstrated his new steam locomotive, "Catch-me-who-can," charging one shilling for passengers to ride around a circular track. But it was George Stephenson, the poor grandson of a Scot who settled in northern England, who earned the title "Father of the Railroad."

Like Telford, Stephenson came from a family of shepherds, although his father was a coal miner. In his youth, he had little or no education, and at age eighteen could neither read nor write. But he was in love with the steam engine, and there was little in the mines that exceeded his capacity to repair. He was one of the inventors of the miner's safety lamps, and in the 1820s built a series of locomotives, the first of which, "Blucher," could pull a 30-ton load up a slight incline at four miles per hour.

Recognizing the importance of education, Stephenson sent his young son, Robert, to a school he could reach only by riding 10 miles each day on a donkey. The father learned to read and write, and took lessons from his son on the latter's return in the evening. Together, they studied volumes of science and technology. Together, as well, they designed dozens of advanced steam engines, each an improvement on the last, and revolutionized transportation in the 1820s. (To complete his formal education, Stephenson sent Robert to the University of Edinburgh, where he studied natural philosophy, mineralogy, and chemistry under a series of outstanding professors.)

In the late-1820s, overcoming fierce resistance from the canal interests and their political supporters, the nascent railroad industry came of age. A cartel of businessmen sought to construct a railroad linking Manchester and Liverpool, thereby reducing transit time from 36 hours by canal to 5 or 6 hours. They conducted the now famous "Rainhill Trials" in October 1829, offering a prize of 500 pounds sterling for the winning locomotive. Paul Johnson writes: the Stephenson's entry, "Rocket," vanquished its competitors by "averaging 14 miles per hour over 60 miles, and it weighed less and consumed less coal than any of the others." In the following year, the Liverpool and Manchester Railway opened, shortly saving Manchester shippers thousands of pounds sterling, as well as offering extensive passenger service. Not surprisingly, shipping and travel by rail became increasingly widespread.

Enlightened Scots and great minds from across Great Britain, many educated at the University of Edinburgh, were transforming British material life. Small wonder that a bemused Samuel Johnson would exclaim: "The age is running mad after innovation; all the business of the world is to be done in a new way."

The question is: What were the practical consequences in terms of living standards and life expectancies of such technological advance?

RISING LIVING STANDARDS — AND THEIR ECONOMIC CAUSE

Economists draw a critical distinction between nominal (or monetary) wages — and real wages. Nominal (in name only) wages are an individual's earnings measured exclusively in monetary terms. So, for example, if a man makes $10.00 an hour, then his nominal wage over the course of a 40-hour work week is $400.00. As a general rule, it is obviously better to earn a higher nominal wage than a lower one. *But in itself a man's monetary wage is an enormously secondary factor in determining his living standard.* For he might make five million dollars an hour and be poor; if, for example, a loaf of bread costs a trillion dollars — as when governments hyper-inflate the money supply, e.g., in Germany during the 1920s, in current Zimbabwe, and in other ill-starred lands.

The all-important point regarding wages is not how high they are — but how high they are relative to prices. It is not how much an individual earns that is central to his living standard — but how much he can buy with his earnings.

Real wages represent an individual's income measured in terms of purchasing power — how many life-enhancing goods and services his money can buy in the marketplace. Afterall, wealth is not money; wealth is goods. The amount of money a man possesses is not central to his living standards. For example, can he eat or wear or live in dollar bills or gold? What is central to his material well-being is the amount of food, shelter, clothing, transportation, medicine, etc., that he can obtain in exchange for his money. If money, not goods, were wealth, the government could ensure universal prosperity by printing and distributing trillions of dollars — but such method does not work; it is the essence of inflation, and it raises merely prices, not the supply of goods and services.

There is only one method to generate sweeping prosperity in a specific nation or across the globe: create a colossal supply of consumer goods relative to demand for them, which thereby lowers the price of vital goods and facilitates rising real wages.

The only way to accomplish this is to vastly increase men's productive power. They must produce enormously more of the goods required by their lives than they previously could. The way this is done is by advances in theoretical science, applied science, and technology — and their application, in the form of industrialization, to the production of consumer goods.

Economic science predicts that the production of an immensely increased quantity of consumer goods — a burgeoning supply relative to demand for it — will consequently lower prices, raise real income, and generate higher living standards. The British Industrial Revolution vastly increased the amount of consumer goods. What was its impact on men's living standards?

Today, early in the 21st century, after almost a hundred years of wrangling, economic historians have arrived at a verdict. For much of the 20th century, debate raged between the "optimists" — those who claimed that industrialization raised workers' living standards—and the "pessimists"—those who maintained it lowered them. The debate is over.

Statistical analysis conducted by economic historians show significant gains for virtually all types of workers during this era. Overall improvement for the period stretching from 1781-1851 show an average real wage gain in excess of 60 percent for farm workers, over 86 percent for blue collar workers, and more than 140 percent for all workers, including white collar ones. Such leading economic historians as Peter Lindert and Jeffrey Williamson point out: "The evidence suggests that material gains were even bigger after 1820 than optimists had previously claimed…"

Williamson concludes: "After a prolonged stagnation [stretching for centuries during the pre-capitalist, pre-industrial eras], blue-collar workers' real wages doubled between 1810 and 1850. This is a far larger increase than even past optimists had announced…the debate over real wages in the early 19th century is over: the average worker was much better off in any decade from the 1830s on than in any decade before 1820." Though researchers tend to be cautious regarding broad generalizations from empirical data, one economist now claims the evidence is "overwhelming" that workers' real wages rose as a result of Britain's Industrial Revolution.

The critics of capitalism who follow the teachings of Marx often make the error of believing that a worker, because he sells his labor to an employer, is therefore not working for himself. That he works for his employer who hopes to significantly profit, in part from his labor, is clear. But what is often missed is that he receives far more than his monetary wage in return. Because the system of mass production creates an abundance of goods inexpensively, his wages purchase an increased amount of food, coal, clothing, etc. He and his family consequently have more to eat, newer and cleaner clothes to wear, and more fuel with which to heat their homes and cook their food. Increased production has its counterpart in a generalized increased consumption, including by the workers. In an important sense, he works for himself—for his own gain and betterment.

The great Austrian thinker, Ludwig von Mises, perhaps the 20th century's preeminent economist, points out: "The outstanding fact about the Industrial Revolution is that it opened an age of mass production for the needs of the masses. The wage earners are no longer toiling merely for other people's well-being [as a serf on a feudal manor.] They themselves are the main consumers of the products the factories turn out. Big business depends on mass consumption."

There are laws of nature—in economics, as well as in physics. Just as it is not possible for a man to step off the observation deck of the Empire State Building and fly to Europe by flapping his arms, so it is not possible to greatly increase the supply of consumer goods relative to demand and thereby diminish the general living standards of men in a free society. Be clear: these are not unlikely occurrences—they are impossible. It is well in this regard to remember the famous exhortation of the great 19th century French economist,

Jean-Baptiste Say: "Produce, produce, that is the whole thing!"

These facts of economic history are fully congruent with the principles—and predictions—of economic science. Taken together, they provide an integrated understanding that and how living standards are greatly increased among persons previously suffering in desperate poverty.

A related point: capitalism's critics often blame capitalism for the inhuman poverty of the factory workers during the system's early days. This is to commit the logical fallacy of context dropping. No phenomenon can be understood independent of the causal factors that give rise to it. The heartbreaking destitution of the European masses prior to the Industrial Revolution has been thoroughly documented—a penury universal minus a relative handful of aristocrats and their favored supplicants; *a penury initiated and sustained by feudalism and its legacy, and inherited by capitalism upon its historic emergence in the late-18th century.*

To ignore this is to sweep aside the facts of such destitution's genesis. To then accuse capitalism of causing the poverty, while in the very act of eradicating it—and, historically, quickly—is to commit both a logical fallacy and a profound injustice; one that, by undercutting support for capitalism, diminishes the only hope of the world's poor to rise into middle class affluence.

In brief: the European masses subsisted at or near the starvation level for well over a thousand years. Capitalism immensely raised their living standards in a century.

Further, rising real wages in the capitalist nations put a definitive end to the primitive practice of child labor. For centuries prior to capitalism, children had performed grueling labor in the fields or cottage industries; in capitalism's early days, they toiled in the factories. The reason for this is manifest: parents were too poor to support the children; in many cases, could not support themselves. Children labored, literally, in order to eat. The rising real wages of industrial capitalism meant that for the first time in history, millions of parents could provide for children with no need of the young supplying income.

To legislate against child labor in the absence of rising real wages would be hideously evil—for it would condemn to starvation untold thousands, probably millions, of desperately poor children. Today, child labor exists throughout—and only in—the non-capitalist Third World, because its lack of technological advance renders it impossible to create vast supplies of consumer goods, and consequently impossible for millions of parents to financially provide for their children.

Not surprisingly, life expectancies began to rise during the Industrial Revolution, finally climbing higher than the mid-30s, near which they had stagnated for centuries. For example, according to E.A. Wrigley and R. S. Schofield, Britain's leading demographers of this period, in 1541, the English life expectancy was 33.75 years. It rose and fell thereafter within a limited range—but in 1761, on the eve of the Industrial Revolution it was still merely 34.23 years. *It had increased, on average, by less than one-half year in great-*

er than two centuries.

By contrast, in 1811, it was 37.59; in 1851, it had climbed to 39.54; and in 1871, to 41.31. *During the Industrial Revolution, the average expectancy of life increased by greater than seven years in just over a century.* By the turn of the 19th century, the trend was clearly upward. Eminent American economist, Julian Simon, edited a massive compendium, *The State of Humanity*, which chronicles this rise and its reasons. "It is clear that a steady advance begins just after the turn of the 19th century, and accelerates after about 1871-5."

The pre-industrial period could generate only minor fluctuations in life expectancy, averaging in the mid-to-high 30s, but the Industrial Revolution created a sustained upward movement. Leading economic historian, R.M. Hartwell, points out: "People lived longer because they were better nourished and sheltered, and cleaner, and thus were less vulnerable to infectious…diseases…that were peculiarly susceptible to improved living standards." Again from Simon's book—a profound point upon which to ruminate: "It took thousands of years to increase life expectancy at birth from just over 20 years to the high 20s. Then in just the past two centuries, the length of life…in the advanced [i.e., industrialized] countries jumped from less than 30 years to perhaps 75 years."

The bottom line regarding practical affairs is that people lived longer at higher living standards. Peter Gay, the leading modern scholar of the Enlightenment, tells us: The men of this period "experienced an expansive sense of power over nature…the pitiless cycles of epidemics, famines, risky life and early death…the treadmill of human existence—seemed to be yielding at last to the application of critical intelligence." It was in this period, because of its deepest premises and values—its commitment to "inquiry and criticism," to independent rational thought—that Gay concludes Western man enjoyed a "recovery of nerve."

A key element of such recovery is that given the principle of individual rights, men not only lived longer, *they lived freer*, i.e., they were legally liberated to pursue their own interests, their own loves, their own values, their own happiness. Human life was becoming better and longer, both qualitatively and quantitatively.

THE PHILOSOPHIC REASONS FOR ADVANCE

These can be stated simply and succinctly. The principle of individual rights maintains that a man's life belongs not to God or to the state—but to him. It thereby liberates men to pursue their own happiness. In liberating individuals to pursue their own wellbeing it thereby protects the best among mankind: those most conscientiously devoted to the use of their minds.

The life of James Watt, for example—or Joseph Priestly or Thomas Telford or one of a thousand other innovators—no longer belongs to the king or the feudal baron or the Church. It belongs to him. Given his fascination with knowledge, with education, and specifically with the practical properties of steam power, he is now free to study these phenomena, to gain a deepened understanding of them, to invent a contrivance to apply this understanding in practice, to enter into partnership with Matthew Boulton, to manufacture the steam engine, to perfect it, to sell them to the rising class of entrepreneurs and industrialists, to amass a well-earned fortune, etc.

If a government legally protects an individual's right to his own life, it does, in that very act, protect his right to his own mind. Those most dedicated to thinking independently, to developing original ideas, to discovering new knowledge, to inventing novel products, etc., are thereby liberated to do so. This is why, historically, when the principle of individual rights first gained cultural currency in Britain and America during the Age of Reason, the Enlightenment, and their aftermath, the outpouring of advances in multiple fields resembled a miracle in stark contrast to the preceding centuries of stagnation.

In contrast to statism of any and every variant—be it secular or theocratic, medieval or modern, aristocratic or military or Fascist or Communist or other—*under capitalism an intellectually independent man enjoys a corresponding political independence.* If he formulates a revolutionary theory, writes a startlingly original book, invents a new product, poses challenging objections to the secular or religious authority—he requires no permission from state or church to bring his advances to the attention of thinking men.

Under theocracy, for example, Charles Darwin would have been suppressed. Under National Socialism (from which he fled) Albert Einstein would have been executed. Under Communism (from which they fled) such independent minds as Aleksandr Solzhenitsyn and Ayn Rand would have been liquidated. But under capitalism, such doughty freethinkers require courage to risk only their reputations, their wealth, and their careers—not their freedom, their health, or their lives. *An innovator's struggle in a free society is a battle of ideas, not of physical coercion.*

There exists, under capitalism, a free marketplace of ideas, which underlies and gives rise to its burgeoning free marketplace of commodities.

This era demonstrates in the microcosm what laissez-faire capitalism—the system of individual rights—perennially offers mankind: the right to deploy one's mind in service of one's earthly existence—and the life-giving advances that inevitably ensue.

But if the capitalist system could speak, at this historical moment it might have proudly yawped: "You ain't seen nothing yet!" For Britain's cultural progeny, across the pond in North America, in the 19th century wrought the most staggering advances in applied science, technology, and rising living standards that the world has ever witnessed—before or since.

Chapter Three
The Inventive Period

The hallmark of capitalism is an unbreached commitment to the principle of individual rights. Has such a society ever existed in human history? Not yet—but mankind came close to achieving the ideal in the United States of the late 19th century. This period—from the 13th Amendment ending slavery in 1865 until the growing influence of the so-called "Progressives" at the turn of the 20th century, in which government intensified its policy of restricting and regulating productive businesses—constitutes the freest period of the freest nation of history.

In 1902, Attorney General Knox, acting under the orders of President Theodore Roosevelt, announced a federal case designed to break up the Hill-Morgan-Harriman super trust, the Northern Securities Company. Though the great railroad builder, James J. Hill, pointed out that his railroads carried freight at the lowest rates and had helped open the economic development of the Pacific Northwest, the Supreme Court disregarded such facts, ruling in 1904 that Northern Securities stood in violation of the Sherman Anti-Trust Act and had to be broken up. The Northern Securities Case, as a landmark application of the Sherman Act, and of Progressive anti-free market principles more broadly, can be seen symbolically as the end of the era of almost unfettered capitalism in the United States. The movement toward statism, toward increased government control over productive men and their activities—and of an erosion of individual rights—accelerated after this.

But in America during the years between the end of the Civil War and the turn of the 20th century—certainly in the nation's northern states, where legally coerced racial segregation was absent—the government protected men's individual rights more fully and stringently than at any other place or time of history. *This means that the legal initiation of force was at an historic all-time low*. Given recognition of the mind's role in promoting advance, and of its non-negotiable need of freedom, one would predict a torrential outpouring of creative achievements in America's northern states of this era. What, in fact, was the practical result of such freedom?

The 19th century in America was the single greatest era of technological and industrial advance in human history. Americans of this period invented the telegraph, the reaper, and the sewing machine. They created skyscrapers, perfected the suspension bridge, invented the camera, the phonograph, the electric light, the motion picture projector, and, early in the 20th century, the television. Innovative Americans revolutionized transportation by commercializing the automobile and inventing the airplane—and wrought sweeping advance in communication by inventing the telephone. They created vast industries in steel and oil and constructed a transcontinental railroad. In manufacturing, they developed the method of assembly line production that brought modern inventions to millions. Such advances, and others, immensely raised the country's living standards—and, in time, brought progress to large areas of the globe.

The world center of technological progress and industrial development shifted from Great Britain to the United States in the final third of the 19th century. In effect, although the technological and industrial revolutions were born in Britain, they reached their full fruition in America.

A MONUMENTAL OUTPOURING OF GENIUS

A brief survey of the period makes clear its extraordinary achievements. For example, Thomas Edison's (1847-1931) contributions are legendary. His first great creation was the quadruplex telegraph in 1874, an improvement on Samuel Morse's (1791-1872) telegraph, itself a superlative innovation of 19th century America. The quadruplex permitted multiple messages to be sent in the same direction simultaneously over the same wire.

Edison continued his singular career with the invention of the phonograph (1877), the incandescent light (1879), the electric power plant (1882), the motion picture camera (1893), the storage battery (1909), and numerous other devices. This greatest of all inventors, a productive fiend, once said of himself that he had worked 18 hours a day for 45 years. When he was age 75, his wife cut down on his work time—she permitted him to work only 16 hours per day. Once when asked regarding pay and work conditions by a prospective employee, he responded: "We don't pay anything and we work all the time." (Imagine the reaction of a modern union leader to this.) If he had attained nothing else, his magnificent achievement of harnessing electricity to illuminate men's cities was sufficient to render him immortal. He is a giant of applied intellect. But superlative though his contributions were, Edison had comrades in promoting the country's technological advance.

Alexander Graham Bell (1847-1922), invented the telephone in 1876, a device soon to revolutionize the field of communication. Bell, a Scottish immigrant who taught at his father's school for the deaf in Boston, applied for a patent a scant two hours before rival inventor, Elisha Gray, on February 14, 1876. Though the invention was lauded later that year by no less a scientist than William Thomson (later Lord Kelvin), the newly organized Bell Telephone Association struggled financially. Sixteen months after Bell's invention, there were a mere 778 telephones in use. Discouraged, the inventor and his backers approached Western Union with an offer to sell for $100,000, but the corporation refused. "What use could this company make of an electrical toy?" the firm's president snorted. Two years later, Western Union would have gladly paid $25,000,000 for the patent rights.

Gardiner Greene Hubbard, Bell's father-in-law, helped organize the Bell Telephone Company in 1877, a firm that eventually morphed into the telecommunications giant, AT&T. It took almost 40 years, but, finally, in 1915, the first transcontinental telephone line was completed. Bell, in the East, spoke to his old research assistant, Thomas Watson, on the West Coast. He repeated his by-then famous first words over the telephone: "Mr. Watson, please come here. I want you." Watson replied: "It would take me a week now." Bell's invention was making possible instantaneous global verbal communication.

In less than a decade following the telephone's creation, the distinctively American architectural form of the skyscraper was born in Chicago. One practical factor providing impetus to the new mode of construction was the catastrophic Chicago Fire which raged between October 8th and 10th of 1871, burning 18,000 buildings to the ground. The bustling town on the shores of Lake Michigan was only further energized by the disaster. Such historians as Daniel Boorstin and Paul Johnson vividly chronicle subsequent events. The Midwestern metropolis has been described as "the only great city in the world to which all of the citizens have come for the avowed purpose of making money." Appropriately, commercial Chicago then saw "architects descend on the stricken city from all directions," for large areas had to be completely rebuilt and tall buildings could be hugely profitable in "big, concentrated commercial city centers."

The problem of elevators had already been solved by Elisha Graves Otis (1811-1861), whose earlier invention of a safety device removed the hazard from ascent and descent. Otis established a factory in Yonkers, New York, and shortly before his death in 1861 patented and manufactured his steam elevator. The problem of creating inexpensive steel for construction was resolved by Andrew Carnegie, whose vast production was based on enormous new economies of scale. Carnegie employed "larger plants, greater economies, the regular replacement of older equipment by the newest—costing less to operate—and new methods." Such innovations in steel manufacturing increased production, lowered costs, and made towering steel-frame structures affordable to build.

The brilliant engineer, William Lebaron Jenney (1832-1907) erected the 10-story Home Insurance Company Building in 1884-85—with steel girders supplied by Carnegie's firm—the first "building of true skyscraper design or 'cage construction,'" earning him the designation "father of the skyscraper." The renowned architect, Louis Sullivan (1856-1924), worked briefly for Jenney and best represented Chicago's phoenix-like rise from the ashes; in the years from 1887-95, his office received 90 important commissions, including for the 10-story Chicago Auditorium Building, in which he chose to house his own office. The exuberantly confident American spirit created the term "skyscraper," in addition to its practical reality; a January 13, 1889 article in the *Chicago Tribune* was entitled "Chicago's Skyscrapers."

During the years that steel and concrete buildings tall enough to "scrape the sky" were conceived—and at a time when Trinity Church remained the tallest structure in New York City—John Roebling (1806-1869), perfected the design of suspension bridges and began his masterpiece—the Brooklyn Bridge. Roebling, a German immigrant who had studied philosophy with Hegel at Berlin, founded a Trenton, New Jersey plant manufacturing iron wire, which later became the first American firm to produce steel wire rope. According to David McCullough, he was a superlative inventor and "designed every piece of machinery in [his] mill." Known to friends and acquaintances as a "man of iron," he worked inexhaustibly, never owned himself beaten, regarded illness as "a moral offense," and refused to rest. "In all his working life John Roebling had never been known to take a day off." He earned a fortune from the company he created "from nothing"—he was a millionaire in the 1860s—and built bridges and aqueducts across the northeast.

Tragically, Roebling died as a result of an accident that occurred at the outset of the Brooklyn project, but his son, Washington, and daughter-in-law, Emily Warren Roebling, carried the monumental undertaking to fruition. It took the entire decade of the 1870s and cost Washington Roebling years of intense suffering from a severe case of caisson's disease, but by 1883 the epic struggle had been won and the world's biggest, longest, busiest suspension bridge was opened to traffic.

The bridge greatly expedited traffic across the East River between the two growing cities of Brooklyn and New York, handling 37,000 people daily by the time it was a year old and one-half million per day 25 years later. Today, more than 125 years after its completion, the refurbished bridge carries in excess of 121,000 cars and trucks a day. According to the engineers responsible for its upkeep, with normal maintenance the great bridge will last another century. But, they say, if parts are replaced from time to time—"it will last forever."

Roebling's achievement with the Brooklyn Bridge is famous, but today we rarely hear mentioned many of the era's innovative thinkers who invented life-enhancing devices and thereby carried mankind to new levels of prosperity. During the 1830s, for example, Cyrus McCormick (1809-1884), invented an improved reaping machine in Virginia. McCormick was unrelenting. When local farmers showed little interest in his innovation, he canvassed the Midwest with greater success. When sales of his machine were slow, he introduced new marketing methods, including warranties and public demonstrations. The fearsome blaze that destroyed his Chicago factory left him undaunted: he immediately laid plans for new, more expansive facilities. He opened a temporary factory office the following day, and followed this shortly with a provisional manufacturing plant. McCormick was hardly the only manufacturer working on improved farm equipment, but his career provides an excellent example of the increasing "technologization" of American agriculture, with its consequent higher yield and lower price of foodstuffs for all Americans.

The heroic stories of innovative Americans of this period could fill volumes. But briefly: George Eastman (1854-1932), in 1888 revolutionized the field of photography by introducing his Kodak camera, a portable box camera that eliminated the need for expensive, bulky equipment. Science writer, Ira Flatow, states: "In 1900 he introduced the camera that would revolutionize picture taking: the Brownie. Priced at just one dollar, the [small and convenient] Brownie made picture taking so easy even a child could do it." At the turn of the new century, Eastman, a poor young man from Rochester, was a multi-millionaire and the acknowledged leader of a burgeoning industry.

George Westinghouse (1846-1914) acquired more than 400 patents in his career, largely in the railroad industry. In the late-1860s he invented the air brake for trains, a monumental advance enabling massive, high speed freights to stop quickly, thereby averting crashes and saving lives. He founded the Westinghouse Electric Company, hired the brilliant Croatian immigrant, Nikola Tesla (1856-1943), inventor of the AC induction generator, and built the first major AC power plant at Niagara Falls in 1895. Together they demonstrated that alternating current was able to generate electrical power over great distances more economically than the direct current favored by Edison. Because American capitalism provided the freedom to compete, the superior power system won out in the famed "War of the Currents," even against Edison's established name and great reputation.

Elias Howe (1819-1867) invented the sewing machine and—after years of litigation—grew wealthy from royalties on his patent. Isaac Merrit Singer (1811-1875) improved the sewing machine in 1850. The Singer sewing machine was an enormous success, for its inventor was equally innovative as a businessman, introducing such practices as installment buying, advertising campaigns, and service with sales. His improved machine made possible the manufacture of inexpensive clothing for millions, and provided productive employment for untold numbers of penniless immigrants, including many women.

The epic struggle of American entrepreneur, Cyrus Field (1819-1892), to lay the first trans-Atlantic telegraph cable is, unfortunately, no longer widely remembered. From its outset, the enterprise was plagued with disruptions: violent storms scattered the company's ships, the cable repeatedly snapped, the U.S. Civil War intruded on commercial construction. Field's warehouse burned and his company dissolved in bankruptcy. Writer L. Sprague de Camp reminds us that forty times Field criss-crossed the Atlantic, "when such crossings took the better part of a month and were far from comfortable." Finally, in 1866, after 12 million dollars and repeated misfirings, Field and his crew succeeded in laying the transoceanic cable. It made possible quick telegraphic communication between Europe and North America. Oceans, distances, vistas for human beings became neither shorter nor less expansive but were rendered far less daunting, decreasingly insuperable.

As historian Charles Beard observed of America in the decades between 1865 and 1900: "Nearly every year between the close of the civil conflict and the end of the century witnessed some signal achievement in the field of applied science."

On the eve of the 20th century, America's technological advances were only beginning. Though Charles and Frank Duryea of Illinois, who built their first car in Massachusetts in 1893, are often credited as inventing the automobile, engineers in Germany and France had been experimenting with gas powered cars for several years before that. But it was Henry Ford who made the new means of transportation commercially viable.

On the morning of June 4, 1896, Ford (1863-1947), a machinist by day at the Detroit Electric Company, battered down the brick wall of his rented garage with an axe and drove out his first car, a hand-built product of seven years of night work. He began the Ford Motor Company in 1903 and made the automobile a commercial reality. Though at that time, the auto was a mere plaything of the rich—Woodrow Wilson scornfully (and predictably) termed it the "new symbol of wealth's arrogance"—Ford was determined to cut its manufacturing costs and sell cars to middle class Americans. He abundantly succeeded and soon millions of Americans drove automobiles.

That same year of 1903, Wilbur (1867-1912) and Orville (1871-1948) Wright, two bicycle mechanics from Dayton, Ohio, and self-educated regarding the principles of aeronautical engineering, accomplished the first controlled, powered flight of a heavier-than-air vehicle at Kitty Hawk, North Carolina. Starting in the summer of 1899, the Wrights had been studying aeronautics intensively—poring over Octave Chanute's *Progress in Flying Machines* and other books—and experimenting with flying devices. Both the automotive and aviation ages dawned in early 20th century America as a direct outgrowth of the achievements of the late 19th.

No survey of innovative Americans at the turn of the 20th century, no matter how brief, could be adequate without discussing the greatest agricultural scientist of history: George Washington Carver (1864-1943). Though born a slave in Missouri, orphaned as a child when his mother was shanghaied by nightriders during the Civil War, and plagued with a sickly constitution, he overcame unimaginable obstacles to gain an education. He was hired by the superlative educator, Booker T. Washington, of the Tuskegee Institute for $125.00 per month in 1896 and worked there for 47 years, repeatedly rejecting proffered salary increases with the response: "What would I do with more money? I already have all the earth." He once turned down a job offer from Edison that included an annual salary of $100,000 and a chance to work at state-of-the-art facilities, opting to remain at Tuskegee.

He developed a new type of cotton—Carver's Hybrid—pioneered peanuts, sweet potatoes, and, to a lesser degree, pecans as leading crops, emphasized crop rotation, taught methods of soil improvement, and, by means of his discoveries, induced southern farmers—white and black—to grow crops other than cotton.

In 1940, Carver, a lifelong bachelor, contributed all of his money to the founding of the George Washington Carver Foundation at the Tuskegee Institute for purposes of scientific research. His achievements, impossible if the feudal-agrarian slave system had continued, illustrate not merely that individual rights are necessary for intellectual advance—but, more subtly, that capitalism institutionalizes a culture of dynamic innovativeness that stimulates superlative creativity, including by men who seek their reward in forms other than the monetary. Individualism protects the right of one to pursue a non-commercial dream (including that of a man who pioneered new crops, thereby creating vast amounts of wealth in the form of additional foodstuffs.)

American entrepreneurs and industrialists also contributed monumentally to the wealth creation of the era. Men like Andrew Carnegie, John D. Rockefeller, J.P. Morgan, James J. Hill, Edward H. Harriman, and others wrought spectacular innovations in such fields as steel, oil, and railroading, to name but several. Carnegie and Rockefeller can be discussed as representative examples.

Carnegie (1835-1919) was already successful by the time he went into steel. But his early life as the son of a destitute Scottish immigrant was difficult to the extreme. His life is the classic example of "rags to riches" success, working at age twelve as a factory boy for $1.20 per week, culminating as one of the world's wealthiest men.

He innovated at every level of his working life, starting with a pooling method he devised as a messenger boy to obviate disputes by doling out bonus money in an equitable form. Later, when employed by the railroad, Thomas Woodruff approached him with an original idea for railway sleeping cars in which he immediately discerned merit. He successfully pressed his superiors to adopt the innovation—and his investment in Woodruff's firm was the beginning of Carnegie's fortune.

But his great work was coming. Recognizing that railroads would soon sweep the vast American West, and that they would require immense quantities of iron, he organized the Keystone Bridge Company of Pittsburgh to erect iron railroad bridges to replace the outmoded wooden ones. Carnegie was justly proud that, in contrast to those of wood, not one of his iron bridges ever collapsed.

In the 1860s, he organized another company to manufacture iron rails and two years later established the Pittsburgh Locomotive Works. In 1866, as soon as patent litigation permitted it, he converted his Freedom Iron Company into plants capable of producing the new Bessemer steel. In 1872, after visiting an English Bessemer plant, he realized he needed a new manufacturing facility with modern, state-of-the-art equipment to produce steel in vast quantities. This was the future—and Carnegie early on recognized it. Despite his partners' lack of confidence, Carnegie insisted that they immediately needed to start producing steel. He founded a new enterprise, the Edgar Thomson Steel Company, to do precisely that.

Burton J. Hendrick wrote an early, admiring biography of Carnegie, showing that the steel titan's genius manifested itself in a hundred ways. Carnegie boldly expanded business operations during depressions when others merely sought to ride out the storm. He kept a careful watch over a diverse array of companies, "any one of which could have provided him with a full-time career." He exhibited trenchant insight into human beings and an unsurpassed eye for talent and initiative; "one of his innovations was a system of promotion within the ranks," whereby he sought, cultivated, and rewarded a solitary and singular human trait: productive ability. He was a fiend for cutting cost, delighting in "tearing down antiquated structures and replacing them with new" and was willing to expend significant sums of money "to improve the productive efficiency of his enterprises and thereby reduce his operating costs."

He was first to employ a chemist at the mills to upgrade the quality of cheaper ore. In America he took the lead in deploying open hearth furnaces. He purchased the American rights to a new steelmaking process devised by an English experimenter, Sidney Gilchrist-Thomas, although the prestigious Iron and Steel Institute of London repudiated it. "No one was...more willing to embrace each new business or technological opportunity than Carnegie." A pre-condition of that, of course, was to recognize them.

The adoption of the Bessemer process, for example, was a monumental innovation in the history of steelmaking. Henry Bessemer (1813-1898) was an English inventor-engineer who revolutionized men's method of producing steel. Previously the manufacturing process entailed days of effort and copious quantities of fuel, resulting in a brittle steel costing $300.00 per ton. The Bessemer method injected cold air into the blast furnaces and produced a tougher steel of uniform quality produced in but twenty minutes. The drastic reduction in labor and fuel meant that steel could sell at $50.00 per ton. Bessemer's advance made him the "Father of the Steel Age." Though metallurgists generally deemed the process untenable, Carnegie quickly identified its merit. In concert with his partners, he bought out other steel producers and converted their plants to Bessemer's process. Subsequently, Carnegie's firm developed new methods of making "the process simpler, quicker and cheaper."

Carnegie produced steel for the Brooklyn Bridge, for the New York City subway, for railroads, for the Washington Monument, and for the U.S. Navy. Paul Johnson reminds us that his furnaces produced "nearly one-third of America's output and they set the standards of quality and price." In the three decades from 1870 to 1900 the American production of steel rose from 69,000 tons to greater than 10 million tons per year. Prices, of course, dropped accordingly—steel rails, for example, which were $160 per ton in 1875, cost only $17 per ton in 1898.

Carnegie himself described the "eighth wonder of the world": iron ore, coal, limestone, and manganese mined in diverse geographic locations, then shipped to Pittsburgh and manufactured into "one pound of solid steel...sold for one cent." Such saving spurred construction of every kind in America—including of skyscrapers, office buildings, apartment houses, automobiles and later trucks, railroads, locomotives, ships, tractors, combines, and other farm equipment, etc., to the immense material betterment of virtually every man, woman, and child in the country. A student of history would look far to find another single individual who so contributed to the economic prosperity of his fellow man.

Unless, that is, he turned his gaze from Pittsburgh to Cleveland of that same era—and to the life and work of John D. Rockefeller. Rockefeller (1839-1937) matched Carnegie barrel of oil for ton of steel, and between them they created the indispensable necessities of modern, industrial civilization—building material and fuel.

Rockefeller chose the refining end of the oil business and his adopted home town of Cleveland—with its advantages of Lake port and multiple railroads—as his base. In contrast to the rampant waste of the early oil industry, Rockefeller founded his immense success at Standard Oil on painstaking devotion to detail, to efficiency, to the arduous task of extirpating waste.

He and his partner, Samuel Andrews, sought ways to derive more kerosene per barrel of crude oil. American historian, Burton Folsom, writes that they "searched for uses for the by-products: they used the gasoline for fuel, some of the tars for paving, and shipped the naptha to gas plants. They also sold lubrication oil, vaseline and paraffin for making candles."

Like Carnegie, Rockefeller was a stickler for cutting costs. He built his refineries efficiently and saved on insurance. He employed his own plumbers and "almost halved the cost on labor, pipes, and plumbing material." By buying his own timber, kilns, and wagons he drastically reduced his company's cost on barrels and transport. He plowed his profits back into the business, buying bigger, newer, better equipment, and generating vast economies of scale, i.e., a decrease in cost per unit resulting from mass production. He hired chemists to develop hundreds of new by-products from each barrel of oil, including paint, varnish, and lubricants. "In a classic move, he used the waste... from coal heaps to fuel his refineries..."

He also understood a paradoxical truth that escapes some businessmen and virtually all anti-capitalists: he increased profits by paying higher wages. The point is stark in its simplicity: higher wages gave him the pick of the best workers—the most efficient, the most diligent, the most productive. *A business does not create wealth by employing the cheapest labor force—but the most productive.* By paying top dollar Rockefeller received the most efficient labor force in the country—and dodged diminished productivity from strikes and work slowdowns.

He knew the oil industry—from big picture to trivial detail—better than any man living. Over the years, he brought together a dazzling array of brilliant men whose talents he harmonized into a single cooperative effort. These executives "all recognized that Rockefeller was an expert in management, that he knew the refineries down to the last pipe and vat, that he had full information upon cooperage, shipping, purchasing, buying, and the manufacture of by-products." They knew also that when emergencies struck, Rockefeller left his desk, rolled up his sleeves, and went to work in the plants, yards, and freight cars. John Archbold, a president of Standard Oil, said: "In business we all try to look ahead as far as possible. Some of us think we are pretty able. But Rockefeller always sees a little further ahead than any of us—and then he sees around the corner."

The final result of Rockefeller's genius was inexpensive oil for the common man. By the mid-1880s, Standard Oil controlled 90 percent of America's refining industry and "had pushed the price down from 58 cents to eight cents a gallon." Rockefeller wrote one of his partners: "We must...remember we are refining oil for the poor man and he must have it cheap and good."

Millions were now illuminating their homes for "one cent an hour" with the inexpensive kerosene made available by Standard Oil—and for many Americans "working and reading became after-dark activities" for the first time. Later, Standard's supply of low-priced gasoline played a significant role in Henry Ford's ability to revolutionize America's system of personal transportation.

He gave away hundreds of millions of dollars in philanthropy, including to such worthy causes as education and medical research—but he confounded anti-capitalist moralists, who admired his charity but not his profit-seeking, by proclaiming that he had done vastly more good at Standard Oil than he had ever done in philanthropy. He was right, of course—*for at Standard Oil, he created wealth;* by means of philanthropy, he merely gave it away.

Rockefeller, like Carnegie, was more than a self-made man; he was a creative genius of the material realm. Mankind has long recognized great minds of the spiritual realm—leading artists, writers, philosophers, etc.—as creative geniuses; but has unfortunately not yet recognized their equivalents regarding production of physical commodities. *Material wealth is created, just as is spiritual wealth, and by the same human faculty—mind power. By employment of any rational standard, Carnegie, Rockefeller, and their equals must be judged Productive Geniuses.*

America was a confident young nation—some would say cocky—and none more certain of his own ability than the man who epitomized American inventiveness: Thomas Edison. Mark Twain captured the swaggering spirit of the era. His Connecticut Yankee stated: "I could make anything a body wanted—anything in the world, it didn't make any difference what; and if there wasn't any new-fangled way to make a thing, I could invent one—and do it as easy as rolling off a log."

That, in addition to their advances, these revolutionary thinkers made many errors is not to be doubted. This is certainly true of the great Edison, who, besides being dead wrong regarding the AC vs. DC "war of the currents," spent years and millions of his own dollars futilely attempting to extract iron ore from marginal deposits. The latter venture cost Edison all of the money he had made on his inventions up to that time—and prompted historian, Maury Klein, to remark about him that "no man was so right about so many fundamental things and so wrong about so many others."

But the outstanding point regarding Edison and the others is not their errors—all men make these—but their exemplary accomplishments. They wrought technological and industrial advances that made America the most progressive and prosperous nation in the history of the world.

Errors of the Anti-Capitalist Historians

But what of the intellectuals? How do historians assess this era of unprecedented creativity in applied science and industrialization? Do they celebrate—even recognize—the life-enhancing, indeed revolutionary, nature of the period? Unfortunately, they do not. Employing another Mark Twain line, American historians characteristically refer to the post-Civil War period as the "Gilded Age," as though America's ascent to wealth was inherently corrupt. One writer refers to the era as the "Great Barbecue," to which only a privileged, exploitative few were invited. Often, these same historians dub the major businessmen of the era "robber barons," as if their fortunes were attained by methods fraudulent and venal.

A representative example: Richard Hofstadter, one of the most accomplished of American historians, accepted and perpetuated the rapacious view of 19th century American business. "Under the competitive capitalism of the 19th century," he wrote, "America continued to be an arena for various *grasping* and creative interests." In a chapter entitled, "The Spoilsman: An Age of Cynicism," Professor Hofstadter acknowledged that the country at this time was preeminently in the hands of business entrepreneurs and then proceeded to claim: "The industrialists of the Gilded Age were…parvenus and they behaved with becoming vulgarity; but they were also men of heroic audacity and magnificent exploitative talents—shrewd, energetic, aggressive, rapacious, domineering, insatiable. They directed the proliferation of the country's wealth, they seized its opportunities, they managed its corruption…"

In the same intellectual vein is Matthew Josephson's influential book, *The Robber Barons*. Josephson, an American writer and biographer, began his study of the great American capitalists with the following quote from Bacon: "There are never wanting some persons of violent and undertaking natures, who, so they may have power and business, will take it at any cost." In an updated 1962 Foreword to his book first published in 1934, he stated that attempts to revise the Hofstadter-Josephson view, depicting entrepreneurs as creators rather than plunderers of wealth, recalled "the propaganda schemes used in authoritarian societies, and the 'truth factories' in George Orwell's…1984." The book's content was more of the same.

Predictably, to Josephson, inventors and innovators, when mentioned at all, were not heroic men of genius, but had simply taken from the "reservoir of knowledge which is the general property of human society"—and who themselves were generally "used and flung aside by men of ruse and audacity who had shown gifts for the accumulation of capital..." Simply put, his view was that inventors expropriated to themselves numerous small advances made by many common men, and were then themselves expropriated by wealthy capitalists, who profited hugely from the new creations, leaving the inventor bereft and "displaced," rarely able to "win the full fruits of his invention." (All of this from a man who, in fairness, authored an excellent and admiring biography of Thomas Edison—and who, consequently, should have known better.)

Professor Hofstadter wrote blandly and unquestioningly, as if he could imagine no alternative to this view—that the captains of industry did their work "cynically," and that "exploiting workers...milking farmers, bribing Congressmen, buying legislatures..." was their standard mode of procedure. He took it as self-evident that the leading entrepreneurs of the period stole their wealth. He treated graft and corruption as the dominant essence of the age.

Not surprisingly, then, Thomas Edison was not deemed worthy of inclusion in his chapter on late-19th century America. Alexander Graham Bell was not mentioned. Nor was George Eastman. The incipient studies of the Wright brothers were not included. Nor was mention of Henry Ford's construction of his first automobile. Nor was George Westinghouse's use of alternating current to generate a seething new energy source. Endless claims were made regarding the "rapacity" with which entrepreneurs and industrialists strove for money and power. But the inventions—and the brilliant minds that created them—the new products, the innovations, the mass production of inexpensive consumer goods, the era's rising living standards, none of these were worthy of his notice.

But to those who study economic history, the facts are clear regarding America's extraordinary economic growth. In 1790, there were roughly 4 million people living in the United States; by 1860, the population was 31 million; and by 1900, 84 million. Average American per capita income doubled between the ratification of the Constitution and the outbreak of the Civil War—and then, despite the arrival of millions of penniless European immigrants, doubled again between the conclusion of the Civil War and the outbreak of World War I. In the 19th century's second half, American wage rates were at least twice those offered in Europe. Economist, Jonathan Hughes, writes: "This rise in population, enormous as it was, was actually outstripped by increases in output of goods and services to such an extent that the rising output per head of population came to be a thing taken for granted by Americans." Increasing production of goods and services meant greater supplies, diminishing prices, and the widely rising living standards for which America became justly famous.

As noted above, wealth is goods. Wealth is food, clothing, shelter, medicine, etc. Money is an indispensable means to facilitate the exchange of goods, vastly superior to a crude barter system—but money is not wealth. Wealth is electrical power to generate light and heat, and to power refrigerators, stoves, and air conditioners. Wealth is the capacity to transport yourself quickly and comfortably from one place to another in your personal automobile—or to traverse oceans and continents in a matter of hours by means of air transport. Wealth is the capacity to communicate instantaneously with your loved ones across town or around the globe by means of telecommunication. Wealth is the increased quantity of affordable clothes made possible by electric sewing machines. Wealth is the prodigious quantity of inexpensive food made possible by reapers and other modern agricultural implements.

From whom was this wealth stolen? Who possessed electric light prior to Edison? Who possessed telephones prior to Bell? Who owned automobiles prior to Ford? The accurate answer to these and many similar questions is: nobody. *Prior to any possible form of theft, it is logically necessary that wealth be created.* Who created such wealth? Overwhelmingly the truthful—and just—answer is: American inventors, innovators, entrepreneurs, and industrialists, of whom a glorious handful has just been discussed.

Professor Hofstadter and the other historians of this popular, influential school are profoundly, egregiously, tragically mistaken. The inventors, innovators, entrepreneurs, and industrialists of the period created a vast and dazzling array of new products and methods; their productivity wrought unprecedented prosperity in the United States; their fortunes were abundantly earned.

Fraud and graft are present in any country and era. A coruscating starburst of technological advance is not. The unprecedented progress in applied science is the differentiating characteristic of the age, not the routine presence of social corruption (which is vastly more prevalent and life-strangling under statist regimes than in free countries.) The term "gilded" means to coat with gold, as though to provide a deceptively pleasing outward appearance to a reality profoundly unattractive. But if late-19th century America appeared golden on its surface, it was because its bedrock foundation was 24 carat gold—especially when contrasted with the stupefying stagnation of the prolonged pre-capitalist era antecedent to it.

The designation "Gilded Age" does not merely miss the essence of the era, it distorts and contradicts it. Inventiveness was the dominant characteristic of the age; it must be acknowledged and celebrated. From now on, the era must be glorified for what it was. *It was the Inventive Period.* If Germany is the land of poets and philosophers, as has often been claimed, then the United States is the land of inventors and innovators.

No thinker has understood this vital point as clearly as Ayn Rand. "Throughout the centuries there were men who took first steps down new roads armed with nothing but their own vision. Their goals differed, but they all had this in common: that the step was first, the road new, the vision unborrowed..." Though their inventions, innovative methods, and groundbreaking theories were often opposed by society, "the men of unborrowed vision went ahead. They fought, they suffered and they paid. But they won." In no country is this as true as in the United States. In no era was this as real as during The Inventive Period.

Anti-capitalist historians commit a version of the identical error by vilifying the era's leading businessmen as "Robber Barons." Carnegie, Rockefeller, and other representative entrepreneurs and industrialists of the era are characteristically depicted as swindlers, bullies, and cheats, trampling the rights of the common man in their desperate, headlong rush to larcenous fortunes. Of the period's leading businessmen, it has been claimed by such authors as Vernon Parrington and Daniel Bell: "A note of tough-mindedness marks them. They had stout nippers. They fought their way encased in rhinoceros hides. There was the Wall Street crowd...blackguards for the most part, railway wreckers, cheaters and swindlers, but picturesque in their rascality." Or: "...the iron-jawed capitalists prepared to demonstrate that the philosophy of natural rights meant their God-given authority to rule untrammeled."

Such writing is vivid, robust, picaresque—and resides in intellectual environs impregnably data-free. Such authors treat facts as disposable luxuries, pleasant perhaps, but ultimately of secondary importance to the understanding of capitalism's history, which is to be conceptualized and construed pre-eminently by reference to their dainty, anti-profit, anti-egoist moral code. What are the economic facts of the period? Several have already been adduced— here are more:

During the Inventive Period, American production of anthracite coal increased by 422%--and of bituminous coal by 2,260%; of petroleum by 9,060%; of crude steel by 10,190%. Real wages rose by 20%. Per capita income grew by an average of roughly 3% annually. National wealth displayed a fourfold increase, from $30 billion to greater than $120 billion. *Enormous wealth was created that immensely increased American living standards, despite the influx of millions of penniless European immigrants—indeed, that served as one attracting cause of that influx.*

The great virtue of such productiveness will be discussed in the section on capitalism's moral superiority. But a prior point can be made here, as stated by the distinguished historian, Louis Hacker:

> The "Robber Barons" were not the despoilers we have been led to believe. The United States of the post-Civil War period...was transformed in not more than a single generation into the greatest industrial nation of the world...A complete transportation net, the beginnings of the generation of electrical power...the creation of new industries, the modernization of farm plant: all these were accomplished in this brief time. In consequence all sectors of the economy benefited.

Were there also crooks and cheats and fraudulent connivers? Of course—as in any era or society—as are rampant in politics and other fields, not merely in business. But corruption in business, politics, or elsewhere fails to create a scintilla of wealth and is emphatically not the central storyline of the Inventive Period. America of this era will not be understood if treated akin to a Third World, banana republic dictatorship, where corruption is endemically routine and politicians daily accept bribes from a prostrate populace left no other means of survival.

If raising living standards and promoting human life is the proper goal—as this writer and many others believe—then it must be recognized that the time is long past to jettison the misconceived "Robber Barons" view and to celebrate the leading 19th century entrepreneurs and industrialists for what they were—Productive Geniuses.

What made possible this extraordinary outpouring of creativity and inventiveness? What are the causal factors underlying and giving rise to such dynamic, inexhaustible innovativeness? What factor prevalent in 19th century American society was responsible for the Inventive Period? The answer should be obvious: America was and remains the nation of the Enlightenment.

THE UNDERLYING CAUSES OF THE INVENTIVE PERIOD

Among the revolutionaries responsible for founding the American Republic were leading thinkers of the American Enlightenment, most prominently Benjamin Franklin and Thomas Jefferson—men preeminently dedicated to the inalienable rights of the individual, to the freedom of his mind, and to the mind's application to create life-giving practical advances. It was no accident, after all, that Franklin, equally great a scientist as he was a freedom fighter, felt chagrined until he found some practical use for the knowledge gained from his pioneering experiments with electricity—or that Jefferson, a prodigious scholar, was also an inventor, architect, and discerning writer on Virginia agriculture, climate, geography, and natural history. "On the altar of God," Jefferson stated, "I swear eternal hostility against all forms of tyranny over the mind of man." The attempt to liberate man's mind to improve the practical conditions of his earthly life was of the Enlightenment's essence.

That period's commitment to the practical application of the freethinking mind was a foundational principle of the new republic, one that to the present day informs numerous American institutions. The more obviously practical an endeavor, the more vociferous is American support. Although the Humanities flourish, as would be expected in a free country—for example, in the creation of a superlative body of national literature, in the development of a publishing industry, a music industry, a film industry, and the support in every major city of art museums, ballet troupes, and symphony orchestras—American genius realized its full, protean, unprecedented flowering in the fields of theoretical and applied science, technological advance, and industrialization.

The Americans recognize the practical value of applied science in the way the Greeks recognized philosophy. The American commitment to the material improvement of human life by means of applied mind power has never been equaled by another civilization. It is one key to understanding the unparalleled standard of living reached in the United States.

The other, related key is political-economic freedom. A cultural commitment to applied thought obviously entails an equal commitment to the freedom of the thinkers applying their thought. The leading minds of the Inventive Period were free to develop and openly articulate original ideas, to create revolutionary products, to found new businesses, to seek private investment, to manufacture pioneering devices, to compete with older technologies, to convince customers, to take financial risks, and, potentially, to earn vast fortunes. It was the freedom of 19th century American society that enabled it to become a seething hotbed of progressive ideas and products.

Such original thinkers would be subordinate to the government of a statist regime—be it feudal, theocratic, Fascist, Communist, or another. They would not be free to experiment, to innovate, to create, invent, or market new products. They would have to apply for permission to the potentate, woo his advisors, curry favor at court, abase themselves, and scrape before political power brokers. Now two persons—the entrepreneur and the ruler must agree that the unproven idea is worth trying. When airplanes have never flown, when skyscrapers have never stood, when electric power plants have never lighted a city, people are afraid of such change. The more men that must approve the development of the untried, the more certain it remains untried. The sole means to assure revolutionary progress is to recognize the right of every man—including those ultimately proven cranks, quacks, and flat earth crackpots—to vigorously participate in a free market of ideas and then, similarly, to recognize the right of every individual mind to decide for itself the logical merit of each claim. Two experts in the history of technology—Nathan Rosenberg and L.E. Birdzell—writing of its growth in the West, stated: "The first condition of this proliferation was that the innovations did not require the assent of governmental or religious authorities."

Further, entrepreneurs and coercive regimes hold opposing interests. The entrepreneur gains by upsetting the status quo, by means of "creative destruction," e.g., by filling the highways with automobiles, where previously there had been only horses and buggies (or by building highways where previously had been trackless wilderness). But a statist ruler has vested interest in retaining his power over men. Since the status quo includes his repressive authority, any new development threatening the current state of affairs potentially undermines his unquestioned hegemony. If he recognizes merit in the entrepreneur's proposal, he sees that it will bring increased prosperity to the individual citizen, e.g., owning an automobile raises a man's living standard. But the more prosperous an individual, the more control he exercises over his own life—and the less likely he is to obey an external authority. The statist ruler, forced to choose between progress and power, invariably chooses power. In fact, no statist regime has ever approximated 19th century America for technological progress—and this is a key reason.

But there exists a more fundamental reason that innovation requires freedom and is stifled by statism: inventors and entrepreneurs are independent thinkers, just as surely as are writers, artists, and philosophers. Minds capable of inventing electric light, designing a first skyscraper, or creating and operating vast steel, oil, or software companies are capable of challenging the moral rectitude of a statist regime. *Independent thinkers do not obey.* Dictators of every degree—from Hitler to petty bureaucrats—recognize this and seek to stifle the independent mind.

For example, observe the unending procession of political prisoners in every dictatorship of history, men and women whose only "crime" was to think and speak aloud their forbidden thoughts. The Communists condemned to internal exile the great physicist, Andrei Sakharov, for daring to question the moral probity of the Soviet invasion of Afghanistan. Jewish intellectuals fled the Nazis, who would have gassed them. Mao tse Tung turned loose the Red Guards, a gang of young thugs, to assault, murder, and intimidate into submission China's thinkers, artists, and teachers. The Taliban continue to execute women for the "crime" of seeking an education. Similarly, slave drivers of the antebellum American south legally prohibited black Americans from educating themselves. Numerous dictatorships burn books.

Freedom is fundamentally freedom of the mind. Suppression is, at its foundation, suppression of the mind.

The Inventive Period is one of history's most vivid examples of Ayn Rand's monumental identification that the mind's fullest functioning requires the legal protection of individual rights.

When a society holds a general commitment to reason, it will value freedom as a means of safeguarding the mind's unrestricted functioning. When the men of the mind are protected from the initiation of force, they will carry mankind to advances both revolutionary and undreamed of by generations prior. The 19th century is an eloquent illustration of this principle. America, the freest country of history, rose the highest. Great Britain, the second freest, rose the second highest. The other nations of Western Europe gradually swept away the suppression of the ancient regime, established a degree of freedom surpassed solely by America and Britain, and rose higher than any nation other than these. Conversely, the non-Western countries, lacking an Enlightenment influence, remained autocracies, ruled by kings, emperors, and tribal chiefs. These regions rose scarcely at all—and to the extent they did, by diffusion of Western, primarily American, technology.

The spirit of the Enlightenment imbues capitalism and provides its essence: Free minds, free men, free societies, free markets, free trade.

PROBLEMS OF MANKIND'S MORAL CODE

The fundamental error of virtually all of capitalism's critics, and too many of its supporters, is their failure to understand this absolutely essential point: *capitalism is the revolution, the liberation of creative human mind power from centuries of statism.* The subsequent socialist onslaught against capitalism constitutes a statist counterrevolution against the mind, led fittingly by Marx and his heirs, philosophical materialists who deny the mind's value (even its existence) and exalt manual labor—the work of the body—as the source of economic production; and who uphold statism, in part or in total, to curtail or even to permanently silence the mind's free expression.

An endless succession of facts can be adduced to demonstrate the practical superiority of capitalism to every other political-economic system. But at a certain point, the evidence is overwhelming and the conclusion established. The preceding chapters have chronicled capitalism's all-too-rarely studied history. They have shown the integrity of capitalism's founders and practitioners—the unbreached devotion to inventiveness and progressive innovations manifested by capitalism's heroes. The conclusion of Part One must be: the system of individual rights, in the brief span of two centuries, has wrought greater material improvement in men's lives than all other historic systems combined.

A disturbing question must be raised: why is capitalism assailed by the intellectuals, the moralists, and the politicians? Capitalism's life-giving beneficence is not to be doubted. All those sincerely concerned with human life on earth must fully embrace the sole system magnificently able to promote it. Why, then, do most of the intellectuals oppose it?

Capitalism is condemned solely because it counters mankind's prevailing moral code. Western civilization's dominant morality, in varying forms, for greater than 2000 years, has been the code of self-sacrifice, of dutiful service to God or Society. But capitalism is based in a selfish code of owning one's life, of seeking one's success, of pursuing one's happiness, and of not sacrificing the self. The morality of self-sacrifice and the system of individual rights stand in direct, inexorable conflict. If the facts of capitalism's life-enhancing benevolence oppose men's dominant moral code, it is time to challenge that code.

Part Two
The Moral Superiority of Capitalism

Chapter Four
The Great Disconnect

There exists a paradox in the thinking of most contemporary moralists and intellectuals. Overwhelmingly, the majority are secularists, concerned predominantly, in many cases exclusively, with man's earthly life. They are not religious. Capitalism is the sole system superbly able to advance man's earthly life. Therefore, one would think that they gleefully, joyously, wholeheartedly embrace it. But they do not. The vast majority reject capitalism in favor of socialism. They reject it in favor of this fashionably current version of statism, which, wherever implemented—to the extent it is implemented—abrogates individual rights and spawns poverty. (See Part Three, "The Economic Superiority of Capitalism.")

Why is this? The answer: because morality trumps economics. Moral philosophy underlies and, in application, gives rise to political philosophy. *If men are intellectually consistent, their moral code forms the logical foundation of their political principles.* For example, if a man holds—explicitly or implicitly, consciously or subconsciously, in terms of rigorous thought or as a woozy, half-developed idea—that virtue resides in selfless service to others, then, logically, he is led to the political principle that society as a whole supersedes the individual, and that an individual owes it unremitting service. Any other political conclusion contradicts his ethical foundations.

The name of the moral code stipulating selfless service to others as the criterion of moral virtue is: *altruism*. Virtually all modern moralists are altruists. The name of the political theory upholding the preeminence of the collective, the group, the society over the individual is: *collectivism—or socialism*. To a greater or lesser degree, virtually all modern thinkers are collectivists or socialists—and are so because they are altruists.

Egoism—the moral code upholding the rectitude of self-interest, of pursuing one's own values and loves—is repudiated. *Individualism*—the political theory implementing it, proclaiming an individual's inalienable right to his life, liberty, and pursuit of happiness—is denounced. *Capitalism*—the political-economic system that liberates men to act egoistically by legally protecting their individual rights—is disavowed.

If specific socialist or welfare statist programs are economic failures, even abysmally so, it does not instigate the socialist intellectual to critically re-evaluate his theories, because, designed to enforce an individual's moral obligation to serve others, especially the needy, such programs are, in his judgment, *a resounding moral success independent of economic outcome*. No amount of capitalist success or socialist failure causes him to challenge his premises—because his socialist principles are not upheld on economic grounds but on moral ones.

The logic of the socialist, anti-capitalist thesis is clear: if, in his personal life, a man has unchosen obligations to others—indeed, if the essence of virtue is to provide selfless service to those others—then, in the consideration of social issues, the needs of the public as a whole (others on a grand scale) take precedence over an individual's own hopes, dreams, or values, and it is morally imperative that the government be legally empowered to coerce those recalcitrant individualists too selfish to voluntarily discharge their social responsibilities.

The most influential philosopher of the modern world is the German thinker, Immanuel Kant. Kant was so extreme an advocate of duty, of selfless service, of renunciation of self-interest as the criterion of virtuous action, he claimed that if a man desired to perform an act—no matter if honest, productive, and/or beneficent in outcome—if he derived any personal satisfaction, gain, or happiness—then he could never be certain his action was morally pure; for if he benefited from it, in any form, it might have been performed for selfish motives—and be, therefore, immoral.

To be certain of the moral worth of an act, an individual must perform it in defiance of his personal desires. This was true even of a desire to preserve one's own life. "But if adversities and hopeless sorrows completely take away the relish for life, if an unfortunate man...wishes for death, and yet preserves his life without loving it and from neither inclination [desire] nor fear but from duty—then his maxim has a moral import," i.e., his motive is morally pure.

Though subsequent thinkers disagreed with Kant on a thousand specifics, they generally agreed that virtue required a full divorce of morality and self-interest. "The absence of all egoistic motivation is, therefore, the criterion of an action of moral worth," taught German philosopher, Arthur Schopenhauer.

An example from a recent, widely used textbook in nursing ethics illustrates the extent to which this doctrine has become entrenched. As an illustration of a serious moral dilemma, the authors present the following case: "Let us consider the question, 'Should a person with two healthy kidneys be *forced to donate* one of them to an otherwise healthy person who is in irreversible kidney failure?'...Any person seriously approaching the problem of whether a healthy person should be *forced to donate* a kidney will be puzzled." (Emphasis added.) The rest of the discussion proceeds in similar vein.

The creed of self-sacrifice is so deeply ensconced that a question can be raised seriously whether an innocent person is morally obligated to donate a kidney and, consequently, whether he can be properly "forced" to do so. Most Americans appropriately recoil in horror from the manifest injustice of such a proposal—but to authors of moral philosophy textbooks, it is a serious ethical dilemma. Since, according to altruism, it is morally incumbent to sacrifice for others, it logically follows that such a sacrifice of a man's kidney, his body, even his life is included under the principle's rubric and is similarly obligatory. An individual's right to his own kidney, his own body, and his own life, on such a creed, is thereby annulled.

(The sole reason the authors find an answer to such a question "puzzling" is that they retain, in their thinking, some last vestige of respect for the individual and for his inalienable right to his own body and life; they are not consistently altruistic in their convictions; they hold morally mixed premises.)

On the altruist premises that dominate modern moral reasoning, it is impossible to understand, much less appreciate, the enormity of capitalism's beneficence. Human beings are rational animals; we hold ideas, concepts, principles; above all, moral principles—we need morality to guide our choices, our actions, and our relationships. We understand practical events in accordance with the general principles that we hold.

The economist Werner Sombart may have been a Marxist turned Nazi; nevertheless, he was quite right in his claim: "No theory, no history." History is not a mere recounting of names, dates, and events; it necessarily includes an understanding of them, of the causes of world-shaking occurrences, of the reasons for momentous social change—and for this, men need theory, above all, philosophical theory. What is true of history is similarly true of other cognitive disciplines.

Contemporary intellectuals approach the modern world with an altruist moral theory firmly entrenched in their minds. They look at the Western world of the past two centuries—and it is possible that on the periphery of their consciousness they register the growth of political liberty and the explosion of life-advancing technologies to which it led. But it is hazy to them, at best—they rarely, if ever, acknowledge or write of it; remember, for example, the American historians' standard interpretation of late-19th century America as a corruption-riddled "Gilded Age." What they see overwhelmingly is individuals pursuing profit—seeking wealth, success, personal happiness—eschewing self-sacrifice, unchosen social obligations, and the supremacy of the state—and, hearts breaking, they emit their piteous wail: "It's selfish!"

There is a Great Disconnect between the facts of capitalism's life-sustaining freedom and wealth creation—and the ethical assessment of it by modern intellectuals and moralists. Altruists are intellectually unequipped to identify capitalism's virtues—this is why, repeatedly, they fail to.

The author has been present at numerous faculty discussions or colloquia in which altruist intellectuals point to endemic human slavery in Sudan, to the forced labor of political prisoners in China, to the coercing of workers at gunpoint into factories in Vietnam, and/or to other similarly hideous crimes—and declaim in genuine horror: "We have global capitalism, look at its result!"

In truth, such atrocities represent massive violations of individual rights, are perpetrated in societies that have not, as yet, formulated the slightest hint of a moral code protecting such rights, and, in thereby abrogating capitalism's defining principle, constitute illustrations not of the system's implementation but of its antipode. How then—or why—do intelligent, informed, educated persons, *in all sincerity*, believe capitalism is responsible for these and numerous similar abominations?

The fundamental reason involves a logical application of their moral code. They recognize that capitalism involves the pursuit of profit and that this is egoistic, i.e., self-interested activity. As altruists, they hold that self-interested action entails the victimization of innocent others—such a belief is a key reason they reject egoism in favor of altruism. *Their minds perform, consciously or subconsciously, a rigorous act of deductive logic: capitalism entails egoistic behavior—egoistic behavior necessitates the exploitation of innocent others—therefore, capitalism necessitates the exploitation of innocent others.* They proceed to interpret world events through the intellectual prism of their moral convictions, tragically overlooking—literally not seeing—that a consistent, universal application of the principle of individual rights is the cure for, not the cause of the problem.

Observe over and again that the criticisms directed against capitalism, whether from a secular or a religious orientation, proceed from a rejection of the morality of self-interest. Marx and Engels, for example, wrote: "The bourgeoisie [the middle-class practitioners and supporters of capitalism]…has left remaining no other bond between man and man than naked self-interest and callous 'cash payment'…In one word, for exploitation veiled by religious and political illusions [the bourgeoisie] has substituted naked, shameful, direct, brutal exploitation."

Similarly, Pope Paul VI in the encyclical, *Populorum Progressio*, claimed: "But it is unfortunate that on these new conditions of society a system has been constructed which considers profit as the key motive for economic progress, competiton as the supreme law of economics, and private ownership of the means of production as an absolute right that has no limits and carries no corresponding social obligation."

Thinkers consistent in their disavowal of egoism and upholding of altruism are led inexorably to a repudiation of individualism-capitalism and an embracing of collectivism-socialism.

Political collectivism or socialism is the logical application of altruist morality to social issues. Altruism is a broad moral theory; in proclaiming others before self, it applies to a sweeping range of instances, upholding a man's sacrifice for his family, friends, neighbors, colleagues, acquaintances, and even strangers. *Collectivism is a specific application of an altruist ethic—it stipu-*

lates, in a distinctively political context, the unchosen duty of the individual to the state.

A rejection of an individual's right to his own life—and fervent espousal of his unstinting, unchosen obligations to others—form the unwavering moral bedrock of any collectivist system. It matters not if the regime is Fascist, National Socialist, or Communist—its undergirding moral refrain remains invariant.

Why, for example, did the Nazis proclaim the superiority of the Aryan race? Because, they answered, an Aryan was most willing to sacrifice himself for the people and, therefore, existed at a higher moral plane. As stated by Hitler: "This self-sacrificing will to give one's personal labor and if necessary one's own life for others is most strongly developed in the Aryan...he willingly subordinates his own ego to the life of the community and, if the hour demands, even sacrifices it."

Why did they demonize the Jews? Because, in their view, the Jews lived a purely egoistic existence, unwilling to sacrifice for the people. Hitler again: "In the Jewish people the will to self-sacrifice does not go beyond the individual's naked instinct of self-preservation...His [the Jew's] sense of sacrifice is only apparent...Here again the Jew is led by nothing but the naked egoism of the individual..."

Werner Sombart proclaimed that "a new spirit" would "rule mankind." The age of capitalism was finished—German socialism (National Socialism) was the rising power. German socialism, he emphasized, put "the welfare of the whole above the welfare of the individual." German socialism imposes on individuals "no rights but only duties." In keeping with such moral premises, Sombart launched a familiar Nazi attack on Jews. The Jewish spirit was egoistic and capitalistic in essence, the antipode of the German spirit. The English people, held Sombart, possessed such a "Jewish spirit" and it was morally imperative that the German peoples expunge it in all manifestations.

In National Socialist Germany, there were no individuals—merely interconnected fragments of a greater whole. As one Nazi functionary gleefully made the point after several years of Nazi rule: "The only person who is still a private individual in Germany is somebody who is asleep." Stated Propaganda Minister, Joseph Goebbels: "To be a socialist is to submit the I to the thou; socialism is sacrificing the individual to the whole."

In Italy, Fascist leaders built on identical moral foundations. Alfredo Rocco, Marxist turned Fascist theoretician, glorified: "the necessity...of sacrifice, even up to the total immolation of individuals, in behalf of society...For Fascism [in contrast to capitalism] society is the end, individuals the means, and its whole life consists in using individuals as instruments for its social ends."

Hitler made the moral point succinctly: "There will be no license, no free space, in which the individual belongs to himself. This is Socialism—"

The Communists, waging class war—not race war or national war—opposed National Socialism and Fascism on numerous critical specifics. But regarding moral fundamentals, they were and remain identical. An individual's life belongs not to himself but to the state. His moral worth lies solely in sacrificing for the state, the people, the working class, the group. Marxists, too, are brutally succinct in expressing the anti-individualist doctrine that forms the moral core of their system. A slogan of Cambodian Communism stated to individual citizens: "Losing you is not a loss, and keeping you is no specific gain."

Similarly, in China of the late 1960s, Chairman Mao instigated and oversaw a "Great Proletarian Cultural Revolution" that, at minimum, executed tens of thousands of innocent persons and forced millions into slave labor. The Cultural Revolution insatiably and explicitly demanded the sacrifice of countless individuals for the good of the collective.

The ceaseless and unbounded Communist atrocities, resulting globally in *the numbing total of 100 million murders*, are a direct logical consequence of their moral premises, as are those of their intellectual brethren—the Fascists and National Socialists. For if men owe unstinting service to the state, then it is eminently rational that the state be legally empowered to enforce such service. If an individual has no moral right to his own life—if it belongs to the state—then it is logical and just that the state dispose of it in any manner it deems socially necessary—including the enslaved labor and/or execution of any one remotely suspected of opposing its principles or policies.

The principle of inalienable individual rights functions as an indispensable moral safeguard against the legalized coercion—the institutionalized Terror—that the state may unleash on its disarmed citizens. In the absence of such a principle serving as the bedrock foundation of a society's political institutions, there exists neither moral nor legal recourse for innocent individuals against massive force initiated by a statist regime.

As Ayn Rand eloquently observed: "Individual rights are the means of subordinating society to moral law."

The Fascists, National Socialists, and Communists are undiluted collectivists or socialists because they apply consistently, with no mitigation by a shred of respect for individual rights, an undiluted altruism to political issues and realities.

But in the West, especially in America, altruist-collectivist ideals, though deeply entrenched, are heavily diluted by a sincere respect for individual rights ingrained into the culture during the Enlightenment era and because of its principles. The contemporary Western moral code is of mixed premises— part altruist, part egoist; part collectivist, part individualist; part mandating unchosen social obligations, part protecting a man's inalienable right to his own life and pursuit of his own personal happiness.

Therefore, it is logically necessary that Western political systems—including Scandinavia, America, and every other without exceptions—are mixed economy welfare states. Mixed moral premises, applied in actual political practice, necessitate mixed political institutions.

Contemporary belief that America is capitalist and Scandinavian countries socialist is false. They are all mixed economies. Capitalism entails a full protection of individual rights, including in the economic realm, and bans all initiation of force, including by the government. America of the Inventive Period approached very near such an ideal, but, today and for decades past, its government robs honest working men to finance the indigent, breaks up productive companies, seizes men's property by imposing 'eminent domain,'' and perpetrates a thousand similar injustices. America is a wobbling, unsteady, uncertain mixture of freedom and statism.

So are all other Western nations. In Sweden, for example, a heavy preponderance of welfare statism and government economic regulations co-exist side-by-side with elements of individual rights: freedom of speech and of full intellectual expression is protected, as is freedom of religion, and of voting rights; borders are open for dissenters to emigrate; even in the economic realm, elements of freedom persist; for example, Volvo, Saab, Ericsson are privately owned and operated for profit; similarly for thousands of stores and shops—butcher, baker, candlestick maker—that line its cities' streets.

They are all mixed economies, combining capitalist elements with socialist, because, in deeper philosophic terms, they hold mixed moral premises, combining egoist, individualist ideals with altruist, collectivist ones. America was constructed on the deepest Enlightenment foundations of egoism and individualism; for example, Thomas Jefferson's ringing words endorsing an individual's inalienable right to the pursuit of his own happiness are still deeply cherished as part of its heritage; therefore, America contains as part of its mixture the strongest element of freedom and most attenuated form of statism.

Today and for a century past, America has moved from individual rights and capitalism toward socialism because the overwhelming preponderance of her intellectuals, moralists, and politicians hold mixed moral premises heavily favoring the altruist-collectivist component of the hybrid over the egoist-individualist ones.

Eminent American philosopher and educator, John Dewey, for example, admired the moral code of the Soviet Union, which he visited in 1928. Dewey believed that Soviet educators—unlike their American counterparts—were not hampered in the quest for social change by "the egoistic and private ideals and methods inculcated by the institution of private property, profit and acquisitive possession."

Dewey's colleague, Progressive educator, George Counts, also visited the Soviet Union during the Stalin era. Counts similarly bemoaned the individualism and selfishness of American society and admired Soviet teaching methods. Activity in Soviet schools, he enthused, "is activity with a strongly collectivistic bias,"—and: "individual success is completely subordinated to the ideal of serving the state and through the state the working class."

President Franklin Delano Roosevelt denounced successful American businessmen as "economic royalists" and as "privileged princes of…new economic dynasties," whose wealth and power curtailed the freedoms and opportunities of small businessmen, farmers, and workers. FDR's political rhetoric was explicitly anti-capitalist, leaving implicit the anti-selfishness essence of his underlying moral premises. But a future president, Barack Obama, made those premises explicit. Criticizing those who opposed his plan to coercively re-distribute income, Obama opined: "I don't know when...they decided...to make a virtue out of selfishness."

Mr. President: Unfortunately, most men have not yet done so—for they will make a virtue out of selfishness only when they realize such a moral principle underlies, gives rise to, and is logically necessary to protect their sacred right to their own lives, to the wealth they earn, and to the mental and bodily effort by means of which they create that wealth.

Even in America, the virtue of selfishness has never been fully understood, embraced, or celebrated—least of all today.

But in 20th century America there arose a brilliant intellectual champion of egoism, who authored an incisive analysis of moral philosophy's fundamentals, entitled: *The Virtue of Selfishness*, as well as magnificent novels dramatizing her philosophy—*The Fountainhead* and *Atlas Shrugged*. Ayn Rand was the first great philosopher of history to realize that selfishness, properly understood, was an unqualified virtue, that capitalism's greatness and glory rested on it, and that *a moral defense* of capitalism was urgently required—specifically, a moral defense upholding the profound rectitude of egoism.

In Ayn Rand's work, the Great Disconnect between capitalism's superlative reality and its relentlessly negative moral appraisal would be expunged. The Great Disconnect was caused by the unchallenged prevalence of an altruist moral code and could be effaced only by the ascending prominence of a properly egoistic one. Finally, on such an ethical basis, capitalism would be recognized not merely for the life-giving dynamo it was and is—but as the morally ideal social system.

Chapter Five
The Virtue of Selfishness

Selfishness, according to conventional wisdom, is synonymous with using, abusing, and misusing innocent others in order to satisfy one's own goals or desires. The dictionary defines "selfish" as: "being concerned primarily with one's own interests, benefits, welfare, etc., regardless of others."

Note that the commonly held view construes a man's self-interest as either holding no regard for others—at best—or in abusing and victimizing them—at worst. This, as every other point of the conventional moral understanding, must be challenged.

Mere minutes of careful thought are sufficient to refute such a belief. For example, it is very much to an individual's long-term, rational self-interest to have close friends, an intimate romantic relationship, amicable, respectful dealings with neighbors, acquaintances, and colleagues, because these bring into his life affection, closeness, camaraderie, love, and serenity of spirit— priceless possessions for a human being. Is a man's life and level of happiness more fulfilled—or less—because of such intimacy? The overwhelming preponderance of human beings understandably answer: more so.

A further question can be raised: are such positive, happiness-generating relationships advanced by honesty or by dishonesty—by morally upright dealings or by immoral conniving—by respecting the rights of other men or by flouting them? Clearly, by honest, respectful dealings with others.

If a man lies, cheats, and/or steals, he risks apprehension—and fills his life with chronic trepidation regarding the outcome of such vile activity. He makes of mankind's noblest members—those scrupulously honest—his enemies; and of their most life-supporting characteristic—discerning intelligence—his gravest threat. But if, on the other hand, he works hard, honestly, and to optimal capacity, he earns more than a cheater could ever duplicitously gain, fills his inner life with pride and tranquility, and attracts, as by gravitational tug, persons who venerate a man's supremely priceless possession: strength of character.

Further, when unfailingly respectful toward others, a man stands on unshakeable moral foundations in expecting an identical respect from them. By contrast, if he callously exploits them, upon what moral principle will he stand in demanding justice toward himself?

Such points are readily explainable to elementary school children—how then, do moralists so often miss them? Why does the conventional code blandly, as if upholding an inarguably exact moral axiom, support the preposterous notion that true selfishness—happiness-invoking, *genuinely selfish behavior*—entails the victimization of others?

This is a profoundly important question—and its answer penetrates to the core of moral philosophy. A first part of an answer is to explain what an authentic egoism or selfishness properly entails—what it is and what, in action, it looks like.

In the author's judgment, Ayn Rand has revolutionized mankind's understanding of moral philosophy and is so far ahead of her time that only today, 53 years after the publication of her magnum opus, *Atlas Shrugged*, are professional philosophers finally beginning to seriously study her theories.

The Nature of Values

The key concept in Rand's validation of egoism is: *values*. Indeed, for Ayn Rand, *values are the meaning of life*. What are they?

Values are those things and/or persons that fill a man's life with significance and purpose, those things he considers worthy, valuable, important, the things he is willing to work for, to get or to keep. In her words: "Value is that which one acts to gain and/or keep." Perhaps the key term in that definition is "acts." Values are always the object of an action. Whether a person loves his career or education or money or art or a beautiful home or a particular man or woman or children or any and all of the above—or something other—his values are those things he considers sufficiently important to impel him to purposeful, goal-directed action. Values must be carefully distinguished from dreams, wishes, and fantasies.

Rand's theory is one that proudly upholds personal values and a life filled with the things and persons an individual loves. For example, an individual might esteem an education in computer science (or in biology, literature, nursing, etc.), or a career in teaching (or in finance or in engineering or in one of a hundred other fields), or a romantic relationship with a particular man or woman, or starting a family and rearing children, or one of a thousand other life-affirming goals. Whatever positive, life-advancing purposes an individual holds, he should indefatigably pursue them. Human beings, Rand argues, should seek their own happiness. They are not obligated to serve the needs of their family, to offer selfless service to God, or to sacrifice for society. They should not renounce personal values. Rather, they should live and act self-ishly.

To be self-ish, in Rand's theory, is not to maliciously victimize other human beings, but to hold and pursue meaningful, life-enhancing values. This is what, *in fact*, benefits a man's life; such a life—and only such a life—is in his actual self-interest.

If a man were to be truly unselfish, and actually attempt to practice a self-sacrifice code, then he would have to renounce his personal values; the more urgent the value(s) he surrendered, the more "noble" is his sacrifice considered. So, for example, if a young man surrenders the woman he loves to satisfy his mother's expectations, by these standards he is virtuous; if he additionally relinquishes career aspirations, his own apartment, and an independent life to stay home and care for her, the conventional code deems him even more "saintly." But after sacrificing his love, his career, and his autonomy, his life will be empty, drained of personal meaning, filled with only resentment and bitterness.

An actual sacrifice involves the surrender of a cherished value. If what a man relinquishes is of little or no value to him, it is not a sacrifice. Similarly, if that which he dispenses is of lesser value to him than any corresponding gain, it is likewise not a sacrifice. If, for example, he spends his money on food for his child, rather than on a new car, that is not a sacrifice. But if he spends the money to feed the children of strangers—and permits his child to go hungry—it is. *A sacrifice is the surrender of a greater value for a lesser value or a non-value.*

Most parents understandably love their children vastly more than a new car—the child's well-being is of immensely more importance to them than any conceivable material benefit—and, if the child's health and fulfillment demanded it, they would walk from New York to Los Angeles and back on their knees, and consider they had gained a bargain. Placing their time, their effort, their money in service of the child's welfare above and before any possible material possession is an action that is value-laden; it is utterly egoistic.

Egoism is action in accordance with an individual's hierarchy of values. It means, in Shakespeare's immortal words: "to thine own self be true." In Rand's moral code, a proper and healthy human life involves choosing, pursuing, earning, and never relinquishing values that provide life with meaning, purpose, and passion. To be true to the self—to be *self-ish* in a literal sense—is to be true to one's values.

A further example: an individual might seek physical fitness and maintenance of long-term health. In pursuit of such goals, he exercises strenuously and regularly; he eats nutritious food; and is abstemious regarding such deleterious substances as alcohol, tobacco, and high-calorie, low-nutrition "junk food." It is true that he gives up specific pleasures, say, of eating ice cream or chocolate cake regularly. But to him, fitness, optimal weight, and long-term health are of immeasurably greater worth; his actions are value driven; they are egoistic, not sacrificial—for they gain his most cherished value(s), they do not surrender them.

Egoism entails holding values, prioritizing their importance, and living one's life in accordance with such a hierarchy. Top value gets top claim on time, money, and concentrated effort.

Both egoism's supporters and its critics often construe self-interest too narrowly, considering only financial gain as to a man's benefit. It is true that wealth—earned by honest, productive effort—is an immense value, offering, in myriad forms, potentially enormous boon to an individual's life. But wealth is hardly the only good a man can attain. For example, bodily health, mental health, wisdom, fulfilling career, serenity of spirit, friendship, romantic love, and family, to mention but several, likewise represent significant gain. Egoism is not a narrow moral code specifically urging a man to earn affluence, although such a value is definitely included under its rubric; rather, it is a broader theory exhorting an individual to achieve his values and thereby attain personal happiness. Wealth must be recognized as but one shining value that an honest individual can prospectively attain.

Properly egoistic actions can be observed over and again in real life. For example, a beautiful, charming woman forgoes dalliances with other wooers to marry the man she loves. A serious college student studies for long hours and also holds a job, thereby curtailing elements of his social life, because he works toward a future career of great significance. A young married couple, living in their first apartment, scrimps on vacations and recreation in order to save the money necessary for a down payment on a house of their own. All of these persons and thousands more are true to their values. None of them are willing to undermine or betray that which is of utmost importance to them. All of them are, in Ayn Rand's sense, properly selfish.

Rand's egoism is a revolutionary theory—and for most of us, reared as we were under the conventional code, it is shocking. To establish the claims of egoism, it is therefore necessary to ask and answer a constellation of important questions.

THE OBJECTIVITY OF VALUES

What makes something a value? Is a value any thing a person desires—no matter how destructive to self or others? For example, is it true to say that toxic drugs are a value to a drug addict? Is unearned loot a value to a bank robber? Is unstinting social adulation a value to a desperately insecure neurotic? In more philosophical terms, are values utterly *subjective*, determined solely by caprice, desire, or whim? Or, rather, are they *objective*, grounded in the facts of human nature, specifically in mankind's actual survival requirements?

Rand's answer is that values are objective, not subjective; they are grounded in the facts of reality, not in the wishes or desires of human beings, either individually or socially. The explanation of this point provides a validation of egoism and a refutation of any school upholding the moral rectitude of human sacrifice.

Historically, the question has often been raised in this form: Is there any relation between values and facts? Or: Are men's judgments of good and evil, right and wrong grounded in the facts of reality—or in some other consideration? For example, the eminent Scottish philosopher, David Hume, argued that there was no discernible relationship between values and facts—and that the claim "X is good" merely described the emotional preference of the speaker for X.

Take an example. If it were said "Working hard to support oneself by honest effort is good," most persons would undoubtedly agree. But what makes it so? Is it good because God wills it—or because society demands it—or because an individual feels that way about his own life—or, alternatively, because some fact(s) of reality require it for human survival and prosperity?

Hume, in a famous analysis, argued that such a judgment is certainly not based in fact, because facts are observable, and it was impossible to observe any fact showing the goodness of self-supporting work. We can, Hume said, see a man working hard, devising a budget, living frugally, paying bills, saving money, etc. But where is the "good" in this? It cannot be seen, tasted, touched—or sensed in any other form; it is emphatically not a matter of observable fact.

Historically, there are three schools of thought regarding this issue. Religion claims that the source of good is the will of God. Modernist, socialist intellectuals argue that Society is the progenitor of moral beliefs—and that each society construes the good variously. Finally, a school of thought known appropriately as *emotionalism* upholds the view that each person chooses, by emotional preference, what is good or ill—for him.

The major historical schools of thought repudiate a factual basis of men's value judgments. Ayn Rand stands in direct opposition to these theories. Rather, she argues that values exist only because living beings must reach certain ends in order to sustain their lives—and will perish if they do not. Values, she argued, come into existence solely because of the nature of living beings.

Take several examples: a plant must gain sunlight, water, and chemical nutrients from the soil; if it fails in this attempt, it dies. Such requirements of life are set by the immutable laws of nature, and are subject to neither choice nor change.

Similarly, an animal must gain food, favorable climate, and shelter from the elements. A lion must hunt, for example, and if it fails in its quest for food, it will starve. Again, it faces intractable facts of reality insusceptible to choice or preference.

Finally, human beings must grow food, construct dwellings, manufacture clothing, and cure disease. Their lives depend on it. To reach such achievements they must study agricultural science, architecture and engineering, biology, etc., and they must make the advances in philosophy, logic, and theoretical science that underlie such disciplines. Nature confronts man with a single, simple, pitiless alternative: cultivate the mind as a pre-condition to cultivate the soil—study, create, and grow—or die. Man, despite immeasurable intellectual advantages, is accorded no more choice by nature than any other organism. For him, as well, the alternative is stark: attain specific goals—or perish.

Fundamentally, there is a sole alternative in reality—existence or non-existence; and it is faced exclusively by living beings. The sustained existence of inanimate matter does not require the satisfaction of conditions; matter simply is; it changes its forms ceaselessly, but it neither comes into nor goes out of existence. But life requires the attainment of certain ends. If an organism does not succeed in that endeavor, it perishes. Its material constituents endure—but its life is expunged. For example, the pulverizing of a rock and the pulverizing of a man are actions profoundly different in nature, in outcome, and in moral significance. The one merely changes its form—the other relinquishes its life.

Organic beings must reach specific goals in order to sustain their lives. It is because of this fundamental fact—and only because of it—that values come into existence. *Values are that which nature requires of an organism to maintain its life.* Rand states: "It is only the concept of 'Life' that makes the concept of 'Value' possible. It is only to a living entity that things can be good or evil."

Values are, therefore, grounded in fact; they are objective. It is nature—not society, or God, or an individual's own whim that necessitates plants gain water and sunlight, lions gain meat, and that human beings grow crops, build homes and cities, and cure diseases. Such matters are no more open to choice than is gravity. These are unyielding facts of nature.

The good for an organism is that which supports its life. The evil is that which harms or destroys it. For man, therefore, the standard of good and evil, the measuring rod by reference to which right and wrong are judged, is: the requirements of human life. *All that furthers man's earthly life is the good; all that inimical to it, is the evil.*

Plants and animals automatically, inherently, and with no choice on their parts pursue the values that nature sets as a requirement to advance their lives. It is impossible for a plant to refuse to dig its roots into the soil—or for a hungry lion to eschew the hunt. These organisms consistently strive to further their lives; if their knowledge is insufficient or they are overwhelmed by inhospitable conditions they die—but they are incapable of flouting their survival requirements and wreaking their own destruction.

But because man is a rational being, he can understand moral principles and make moral choices. He can choose, for example, between nutritious food and poison—between education and ignorance—between productive work and parasitism off of honest men—between establishing a free society and imposing a dictatorship—between life-sustaining actions and those life-destroying.

Human beings do not automatically, intrinsically, non-volitionally pursue that which advances their lives; they have the capacity to destroy themselves, to commit suicide in a multitude of forms—and quite often they do. They surrender their values to satisfy others—or they imbibe toxic drugs—or they seek gain by deceitful conniving—or they vote for statist politicians—or in one of countless other modes sabotage their own lives and well-being.

Human beings must choose values, they must choose life, they must choose egoism.

It is a significant and immensely overlooked achievement to be an egoist—for it involves a scrupulous devotion to reality, to the survival requirements of human nature, and to positive, life-affirming values.

To be an egoist is to form, cherish, pursue, and never sacrifice life-advancing values.

Values are those persons, objects or relationships that objectively enhance human life and that are accepted by choice. Life necessitates that values be gained. Bare survival requires bare necessities; flourishing, fulfilled, joyously ecstatic life requires a superabundance of values achieved beyond merely those minimal ones requisite to subsistence. Value attainment exists on a continuum: to the degree a man lives—bodily, intellectually, emotionally—to that degree he achieves values. The goal of a rational individual is to live to the exultantly fullest of his capacity.

On the basis of such fundamentals, Rand's validation of egoism is straightforward. Something is good or evil—a value or an anti-value—based on whether it advances or retards an organism's quest for prospering life.

WHO OR WHAT IS ALIVE?

Only individuals are alive; regarding human life, only individual human beings live or die; indeed, at a deeper level, only particulars or entities—individual things—exist. The logical conclusion is that value achievement is a distinctively individual, personal pursuit.

Howard Roark, the brilliant architectural hero of *The Fountainhead*, makes the important point that just as there is no collective stomach to digest food, so there is no collective brain to think. Digesting, thinking, breathing, and all other processes of body and mind, are uniquely individualistic activities. Similarly—among human beings—there is no collective life form to seek or to gain values. Only individuals live or perish. Consequently, the possibility of value pursuit—and its necessity—is, utterly and exceptionlessly, an individualistic function.

Therefore, "man must live for his own sake, neither sacrificing himself to others nor sacrificing others to himself. To live for his own sake means that *the achievement of his own happiness is man's highest moral purpose.*" Life is the *standard* of moral value, but his own happiness must be the *purpose* of each individual's life.

The necessity of individual value achievement in everyday life should be manifest. For example, a man must gain the education he needs, hold a productive job and earn wealth, seek close, trustworthy friends, and gain the intimacy of a romantic relationship—a set of values warranting fulfilled life, and a full absence of which precludes bare survival.

If human beings are to prosper on earth—even survive—they must achieve values. By what primary method will they accomplish this?

RATIONALITY AS MAN'S FUNDAMENTAL MEANS OF SURVIVAL

Billions of human beings existing in the pre-capitalist societies of the feudal past—or in the non-capitalist, statist societies of the present—suffer(ed) under conditions lacking even the barest necessities of life, dying at desperately early ages from an absence of food, medical cures, and/or adequate shelter.

How—by application of what method—do human beings obviate such calamities, create abundance, and achieve flourishing life?

The great heroes of the Scottish Enlightenment and of America's Inventive Period provide an example of the method and a clue to the answer.

James Watt's steam engine made it possible to manufacture a vastly increased supply of consumer goods, first of cotton clothing and subsequently of a variety of life-enhancing commodities. Thomas Edison's advances in electrical engineering—as well as those of George Westinghouse, Nikola Tesla, and others—made it possible to flood men's homes and cities with a robust new source of light and, eventually, to power such life-promoting advances as refrigerators, stoves, electric heat, air conditioners, radios, televisions, etc. The revolution wrought in agricultural science by George Washington Carver and other agronomists—in addition to the advances in agricultural technology pioneered by such men as Cyrus McCormick, John Deere, and others—made it possible to immensely increase the amount of food grown for human consumption.

The fundamental method employed by such innovators and many others, is application to their respective fields of dynamic human brain power. Such pioneers in applied science and technology, as their counterparts in theoretical science, philosophy, and the arts, are thinkers; they are men and women of the mind; they are geniuses.

A central part of Rand's theme in *Atlas Shrugged* is that the rational mind is mankind's fundamental instrument of survival; the mind is the means by which human beings promote their lives on earth; the mind is the primary means by which human beings create values.

Observe that nature endows every species with especial characteristics enabling them to gain survival. Birds, for example, possess wings with which to fly; lions have claws and fangs by means of which to rend their prey; antelopes have foot speed with which to outrace lions; elephants have vast size, gorillas immense strength, and many animals have fur to keep them warm.

These other species survive by physicalistic means—fur, wings, horns, muscles, etc. But physically, man is, comparatively, an unprepossessing figure: he cannot run like a cheetah, fly like a bird, or daunt would-be predators with elephantine size. He cannot physically compete for survival against these other species. Nature endows him with but a single, salient characteristic empowering survival: his intelligence.

The values indispensable to man's life do not antecedently exist in nature, but must be wrought by human effort. Each of these values is a creation of the reasoning mind. One life-giving example is the progress in medicine resulting in trailblazing treatments and such "miraculous" remedies as antibiotics. Such medications and surgical methods must be researched and developed, requiring knowledge of biological science, which entails the rational mind.

Similarly, the construction of human habitation behooves men's knowledge of architecture, as well as of the principles of engineering and mathematics, which necessitates the mind. Further, the food that mankind grows depends on knowledge of agricultural science—how to fertilize the soil, how to irrigate, when to rotate crops, when to let the land lie fallow, how to genetically engineer new food strains, etc—all of which makes incumbent the reasoning mind.

All such advances underscore the important fact that the knowledge necessitated by human survival must be discovered by man; none of it is innate in his consciousness at birth. Painstakingly, across a span of millennia, great thinkers have identified that a wheel can be created; that crops can be grown; that the sun, not the earth, is the center of our solar system; that the Far East can be reached by sailing west; that germs cause disease; that effective surgery entails antiseptic measures; that medications can be created to expunge lethal microbes; that oil can be deployed to heat men's homes and power their vehicles; and that electricity can be harnessed to provide illumination both brilliant and affordable.

Further, such life-enhancing practical achievements are made possible only by prior progress in philosophy and theoretical science that provide men a *rational method* with which to understand the world. For example, Aristotle formulated the rules of proper reasoning, and identified the main errors of faulty thinking—the fallacies of logic. Galileo recognized that advances in and applications of mathematics were central to further human understanding of physics (and the laws of nature more broadly)—and pioneered the employment of quantitative experimentation. Another brilliant scientist, Isaac Newton, laid the foundations of differential and integral calculus, and formulated the universal laws of motion, including his celebrated analysis of gravitation. Such superlative theoretical accomplishments—and other similar advances— laid the intellectual groundwork making possible the monumental progress described above in such applied disciplines as technology and medicine, as well as in agricultural science and in other related fields.

In *The Fountainhead*, Howard Roark succinctly summarizes the cardinal point: "From the simplest necessity to the highest religious abstraction, from the wheel to the skyscraper, everything we are and everything we have comes from a single attribute of man—the function of his reasoning mind."

In *Atlas Shrugged*, the hero articulates—at greater length but no less eloquently—the identical principle. "Man's mind is his basic tool of survival. Life is given to him, survival is not. His body is given to him, its sustenance is not. His mind is given to him, its content is not. To remain alive, he must act, and before he can act he must know the nature and purpose of his action. He cannot obtain his food without a knowledge of food and of the way to obtain it. He cannot dig a ditch—or build a cyclotron—without a knowledge of his aim and of the means to achieve it. To remain alive, he must think."

All that which furthers human life is the good—and, as mankind's survival instrument, rationality is the faculty pre-eminently responsible for doing so. Rational thought, the faculty that creates values and thereby gives life, is the highest good of human existence. The consistently diligent practice of rational thought is, therefore, mankind's principal virtue.

No human characteristic is as selfish as an unbreached rationality—for it, above all, is responsible for the achievements, the creation of values, upon which human life depends.

Rational thinking—not irrational, impulse-driven, emotionalist behavior—is superlatively selfish. The one brings prospering life; the other, premature death.

THE NEGLECTED VIRTUE OF PRODUCTIVENESS

That human survival depends on productivity should be readily apparent. Every value entailed by man's life—from crops to computers, from apartment buildings to antibiotics—must be created by human effort. Although the higher animals find ready-made in nature the necessities of their lives—whether grass, berries, caves, or other creatures on which to prey—human beings cannot sustain themselves in such fashion. They need houses, not burrows or caves; medicines to cure disease; telephones and the Internet for urgent communication; automobiles and jet travel for comfortable transportation; and a thousand other values, all of which need to be invented, discovered, cultivated, produced.

Human beings do not and cannot adapt to their environment. They cannot grow thicker fur in winter and shed it in summer; they do not migrate with the seasons—or hibernate; they cannot crouch for shelter under rocks or amongst the branches of trees. Because it is not their nature to passively accommodate themselves to their milieu, they are not at the mercy of environmental conditions. If blizzards strike them, animals freeze—but men build homes and heat them with gas, oil, or electricity. Similarly, if flood strikes them, animals drown—but men build dams. By constructive achievement, human beings adjust their natural surroundings to themselves.

Since that which furthers man's life is the good, the production of the values on which human life depends is the essence of a moral existence. Values must be created before they may be given away. *It is the production of values, not their charitable distribution to others that is the virtuous, i.e., the life-giving act.* The Productive Geniuses of history—e.g., Andrew Carnegie, John

D. Rockefeller, J.P. Morgan, Bill Gates, among others—are the truly virtuous individuals; not a "saint" of charity like Mother Teresa.

The great producers create the goods and services upon which human life depends; the saint of charity—at best—convinces productive men to voluntarily support the needy; at worst, seeks to inculcate guilt in the producers for their "selfish" lives, and/or to besmirch their names because of their great wealth, and/or to promote governmental initiation of force to impose a welfare state on the producers.

After the Scientific, Technological, and Industrial Revolutions, it should be clear that the mind is the fundamental cause of man's material prosperity. Related, capitalism's critics, starting with Marx and continuing to the present, manifest woefully inadequate understanding of the demanding thought and extensive knowledge required to head a productive business. Most leading anti-capitalists are intellectuals, politicians, or clergymen who have never run a profit-driven enterprise. In reality, a successful entrepreneur, depending on his field, must plan regarding such factors as purchasing, production, marketing, personnel, and a dozen related issues. The larger and more complex an enterprise, the more its success demands its head man step up, shoulder responsibility, and formulate a grand strategy.

It is well to reiterate here the quote regarding Rockefeller's lieutenants: they..."all recognized that Rockefeller was an expert in management, that he knew the refineries down to the last pipe and vat, that he had full information upon cooperage, shipping, purchasing, buying, and the manufacture of by-products." Or from Carnegie's principal biographer regarding the steel titan: "He was the thinker, the one who supplied ideas, inspiration and driving power, who saw far into the future..." This is the kind of in-depth knowledge and grand-scale vision it takes to run an immensely productive company. If the critics of capitalism disbelieve it, let them morph into entrepreneurs and attempt their own success—or, at minimum, ponder scrupulously its requirements.

After Ayn Rand's monumental achievement in *Atlas Shrugged*, it should be clear that such production of wealth represents a profound moral virtue. The industrialists of the Inventive Period and their modern counterparts solved the problem of material production that had plagued mankind for millennia. These men and others like them created prodigious quantities of inexpensive steel, oil, automobiles, computers, medicines, etc., that fueled building and achievement of every kind, enabling the men of the free countries to attain living standards historically unprecedented.

Productiveness is a significant moral virtue; regarding its most able practitioners, therefore, justice behooves men of goodwill to cease the unconscionable demonization, to commence a proper moral reverence, and to gratefully acknowledge the colossal contributions to mankind's material well-being wrought by their efforts.

Values are the enabler and the meaning of life; they must be attained, not surrendered; and such accomplishment entails productive effort, principally rational thought. With these points in mind, it is now possible to analyze—and refute—the schools of ethical thought opposing egoism.

THE MORAL CODES THAT DENY EGOISM

There are two theories that dispute a healthy, life-promoting egoism. One is *altruism*—the code advocating selflessness or self-sacrifice. The other is the view that upholds a counterfeit egoism—an essentially criminal mentality claiming an individual's self-interest entails satisfying desires not by rational thought and productive effort but by victimizing innocent men. Such a code can most appropriately be termed: *cynical exploitativeness*.

Examine them one at a time, altruism first. Should a man sacrifice what is most dear to him—his education, career, spouse or lover, children, closest friends? The ensuing misery—and/or untimely death—would be colossal. What kind of inhuman theory demands this? Is sacrifice, then, limited to secondary matters in a man's life—a few dollars of his wealth, spare moments of his time, a scintilla of his effort? Are such incidentals truly sacrifices—and, if so, does not this utterly trivialize the code of self-sacrifice? Is this what the moral fuss has been about for millennia? Is this what the National Socialists and Communists demand explicitly from men in political practice?

If moralists upheld the rectitude of achieving life's significant values—and urged "sacrifice" of merely tidbits—they would be egoists, not altruists, and blandly unappalled by rational self-interest, profit-seeking, and capitalism. Some are exactly that, without explicit realization of their own egoism.

But those who are not unappalled—who are bitterly scornful of such principles—stand remorselessly opposed to value achievement, personal happiness, individual rights, and capitalism. In name of service to others (or to the state) they uphold sacrifice of personal values—and the devastating misery that inescapably ensues.

This ghastly phenomenon in men's moral lives—this code of skeletal death—is what Ayn Rand identified as "altruism," and to extirpation of this unlivable creed she devoted her intellectual life.

Cynical exploitativeness, although never fashionable among philosophers, lives a night-crawling existence in the blighted depths of human society. It consists of two inter-locking premises: 1. It is to a man's actual self-interest to victimize innocent others and 2. It is morally right to do so. Both claims are inherently, abysmally, fatally false.

Rand points out: "There is a fundamental moral difference between a man who sees his self-interest in production and a man who sees it in robbery." Indeed, there is. One difference lies in social consequences—for both himself and others. The robber victimizes others while the producer benefits himself, and, as a consequence, others, as well. The exploiter seeks to live out a double standard: men must produce in order to survive and prosper—but I don't have to. In pursuing this contradiction, he makes enemies of rational, productive men, and necessarily surrounds himself with fellow scoundrels, the only type of men willing to consort with such as him.

He consequently spends his life sneaking, hiding, concealing the truth, leading a covert, subterranean existence, a desperate man, on the run, seeking respite from the law and society's most honest members. This is a prescription for misery. Why embark on such a path to hell—when a world of shining values can be attained by rational productivity?

A more fundamental point, however, regards not a man's relationship to society—but to nature. Human beings do not reside in a Garden of Eden, where the goods their survival demands exist ready-made for the taking. It is not society that prohibits man's survival as a parasitical non-producer; it is nature. Reality requires man to produce if he is to flourish: the productive person lives in accordance with this fact of nature, but the parasite fights it. It is a battle no man can win. Society incarcerates him—but nature eradicates him when he runs out of victims.

In *The Fountainhead*, architectural hero, Howard Roark, states that human beings, in their quest for survival, have but two possibilities: they can either face nature independently, learning to create values—or they may seek survival parasitically, through the intermediary of independent men. "The creator's concern is the conquest of nature. The parasite's concern is the conquest of men."

The creators and producers reap a harvest of abundance; they can build, grow, construct, achieve, prosper—and in free societies, they do. They need no one else—least of all criminals and other parasites. But parasites need them; like viruses, they feed only off of healthy living tissue; left to their own devices, in the absence of honest victims, they subsist in miserable squalor, if they survive at all. *Viewed in principled terms, therefore, it is clear where a man's actual self-interest lies.*

For example: how much food actually exists today, even in America, the world's wealthiest nation? For what duration of time could that food last? If men chose to end productive work—to cease growing, shipping, and selling food—and to subsist by parasitical means instead, their recourse to robbery and victimization would entail the survival of those most cunning and violent—for all of several additional days. For after the most aggressive brute plundered his final victim of the last morsel on earth, his own process of starvation inexorably ensues.

Considered long-term, as a matter of consistent principle, human well-being requires the creation of values—the *creation of values*, not their plunder. Consequently, a life of honest productivity, and a rejection of parasitism in all forms, is a man's means to flourishing earthly life.

From *Atlas Shrugged*: "Man's life, as required by his nature, is not the life of a mindless brute, of a looting thug or a mooching mystic, but the life of a thinking being—not life by means of force or fraud, but life by means of achievement—not survival at any price, since there's only one price that pays for man's survival: reason."

Altruism urges a man to sacrifice his values to others. Cynical exploitativeness urges him to force and/or bamboozle others to sacrifice their values to him. But, in fact, egoism is a *moral principle*, it is universal; it upholds the need and moral rectitude of every individual to hold cherished values, to strive to realize them by means of honest effort, and to thereby gain personal happiness.

The same moral principle that exhorts a man never to sacrifice his values requires that he never demand sacrifice of others.

Neither altruism nor cynical exploitativeness has outgrown the primitive call for human sacrifice. They differ solely as variations on a theme: regarding the question of who is sacrificed to whom. An altruist claims that self must be sacrificed to others; a cynical exploiter that others be sacrificed to self. But they concur on the cardinal point: a non-sacrificial mode of human life is impossible. Taken together, the two codes constitute a "cannibal morality," necessitating that some men are eaten by others—that some man sacrifices his value(s) to other men.

But in fact, in reality, values are to be attained—not relinquished. Their sacrifice—in any form, for any purpose, to any man—involves a profound moral error. To quote the hero of *Atlas Shrugged*: "I swear by my life and my love of it that I will never live for the sake of another man, nor ask another man to live for mine." This code advocates a non-sacrificial way of life—a life that repudiates both altruism and cynical exploitativeness, both sacrifice of self to others and of others to self.

Many people might recognize the truth of important points already made: that productivity is a moral virtue—that capitalism is immensely productive—and even that egoism, correctly understood, is a proper moral code, and that its two death-dealing antitheses are repugnant. But they still have a question: what about other people? Kindness toward others is a moral virtue. Can egoists be kind? What is the relationship between egoism and legitimate goodwill?

Chapter Six
Egoism as the Necessary Foundation of Goodwill

The governments, the school systems, the universities, and the churches in concert may be thought of as "The Moral Establishment"—the entrenched social institutions formulating and propagating men's moral codes. For at least two millennia the Western world's Moral Establishment has relentlessly urged, in some form, the creed of self-sacrifice.

One pernicious dogma inculcated is that genuine benevolence—attitudes and actions flowing with the "milk of human kindness"—is equivalent to self-sacrifice. Such a belief is a lethal canard that must be extirpated in all of its hideous iterations and supplanted by a rational, life-giving, proper understanding.

Authentic goodwill—a caring magnanimity toward one's fellow human beings—is a superlatively precious characteristic, to be actively promoted in every form and context. What moral fundamentals promote it? And which ones are as certain to efface it as the plague to eradicate living tissue?

Egoism is the sole moral code able to catalyze a legitimate benevolence of man to fellow man. The code of self-sacrifice necessitates not kindly goodwill but its antipode—bitterness, resentment, hostility. Because of the Moral Establishment's indoctrination of mankind with the equation of kindness and self-sacrifice, it is necessary to adduce a constellation of contrary points.

First: *It is eminently possible—indeed, not difficult—to act in such ways that confer benefit on both self and others.* A rational individual, in an undeviating quest for personal happiness can, will, and does act in ways advantageous to both self and other men. For example, a person seeking all-round self-fulfillment desires close friends, romantic love, and perhaps children, because such relationships bring camaraderie, intimacy, and love into his life. He helps his friends, his lover or spouse, his children—and a consequence of this closeness is the happiness he experiences, as well as they, at their improved well-being.

Related: a person pursues a career in a profession regarding which he is passionate, achieving fulfillment, wealth, and pride from productive work conscientiously discharged. All such gains contribute to his own happiness. Does anyone else simultaneously benefit? Certainly. For example, if the field is medicine, then performance of his diligent best will, in many cases, supplant illness with improved health and induce happiness in both patients and those who love them.

Similarly, if he is a teacher, conscientious execution of professional responsibilities brings into his life purpose, a well-earned salary, and pride in significant work well done. The benefit to his students—and to all who love them—is manifest.

A final example: a businessman who manufactures automobiles, or software, or telephone technology, or one of a thousand other commodities. He works scrupulously, to utmost capacity, seeking the largest possible share of a competitive marketplace. His productive work leads to commercial success for the company, personal wealth for himself, pride of having earned every penny—as well as significant satisfaction of customers who prefer his product to that of competitors, increased revenue for shareholders, and remunerative employment for workers.

Such examples could be ceaselessly replicated. The explanatory principle is: *There is no inherent clash between helping self and helping others—it is eminently possible to achieve both.*

But it is intrinsically impossible to both fulfill and sacrifice the self.

It is no more possible to fulfill the self and, in the same action, sacrifice it, than to create a round square. An individual pursues his cherished values—or he surrenders them—but he cannot do both. In the act of attaining his values he can, and often will, benefit others; but he cannot simultaneously achieve and relinquish those values.

Observe a revealing confusion on the part of charity's advocates. They want, let us say, young people to perform volunteer work in a nursing home. On the one hand, they say: "You have duties to society and it is your obligation to help the elderly or the needy…" But thirty seconds later, the self-same advocate might enjoin the youth with the words: "You'll meet extraordinary people, who have done fascinating things in their lives, you'll form close relationships and have experiences you never dreamed possible…"

The first exhortation proceeds from an anti-egoist code, repudiating even the vocabulary of self-fulfillment and personal happiness, upholding an ethic of selfless service. The second is based on an egoist creed, speaking the language of values, honoring the rights of the individual, appealing to his own goals, interests, and aspirations—to his self-interest. The first, if enacted, leads to a lose-win outcome, in which the recipient of a charitable act benefits only at the sacrificial loss of the provider. But the second engenders a win-win result, in which every party to an interaction—not merely some at the expense of others—reaps significant gain.

(Politically, the first leads to governmental legislation that coerces an individual to perform "volunteer" work, whereas the second respects an individual's inalienable right to his own life and honors his freedom of choice.)

Morally, if an individual elects to aid his brothers and sisters, it must be recognized that this is a choice, not an imposed obligation; such an action is performed as a value, not as a duty; the benefactor genuinely cares for the one he succors—and the recipient's proper response is utterance of a sincere "thank you."

Egoism is fully compatible with helping others—it rules out all forms of self-sacrifice.

Practically, regardless what they have been taught, these are the terms upon which an overwhelming preponderance of mankind's best members perform kindly deeds. They have been indoctrinated to equate benevolence with self-sacrifice—and such is their explicit conviction. But implicitly, they desire life, they seek to achieve values, they pursue happiness, and so, they conduct their lives egoistically. In fact, when they perform kindly deeds, they draw fulfillment from doing so, regardless the lip service they confusedly render to self-sacrifice. Implicitly, others represent a value to them, even if they do not consciously articulate it in these terms. They do not perform kindly deeds on the premise that "others are of no value to me—and I help them only because I must, at personal cost to myself."

This truth extends to compassionate treatment of strangers. In fact, human life is the highest value—and many persons recognize it as such. In the absence of evidence to the contrary, they presume strangers to be innocent—in innumerable ways they are ready to help—they conclude the interaction with a handshake, a warm smile, and a sincere "You're welcome" to the proffered gratitude, and they experience a moment's pleasure at the beneficent outcome. They then proceed purposefully in pursuit of their lives' central values.

Second: As a practical point, a man's sacrifice of himself avails other persons nothing. Only his self-development and self-realization has positive consequences. For example, Thomas Edison passionately desired to electrify New York City. Were New Yorkers benefited by his fulfillment or betrayal of that cherished goal? *Value achievement—not value abandonment—benefits human life.* The valuer himself—Edison in this example—gained first and foremost; secondarily, other human beings did, as well.

In contrast, examine the results of abandoning values by considering a previous example—the case of a dutiful son who surrendered his fiancée, his apartment, and an independent life to stay home and care for his mother. Is the mother actually benefited? If it is genuinely a sacrifice on the son's part, his life will be bereft, empty, miserable. What loving parent is gratified by the sight of her child's pain—especially knowing that her unreasonable demands were its cause? No—a conscientious parent is overjoyed by the sight of his/her child's gaining values and achieving happiness, not by the absence of such. A rational human being gains nothing—he only loses—by another's surrender of personal values.

The explanatory principle is: because values are necessary to sustain life, it is their fruition, not their abdication that advances human well-being.

Third: Observe that emotions are automatic, psycho-somatic responses to values in a given set of circumstances. For example, if a man witnesses the woman he loves threatened by thugs he experiences fear; if he sees her hurt, he feels anger toward the perpetrators; if the tale has a happy ending in which she escapes unscathed, he experiences joy and an overwhelming sense of relief.

A second example: on September 11, 2001, many Americans were depressed and/or enraged by the sight of the free country they cherish savagely assaulted by religious zealots who hate every virtue America embodies. Values are always the fundamental; emotions vary accordingly if values are achieved, threatened, harmed, thwarted, etc.

Therefore, an individual's sacrifice of values—a surrender of what he sincerely holds dear—engenders in his life only deprivation, suffering, misery. To reprise an earlier point: Should an individual actually sacrifice what he loves? Should he sacrifice his education, his mind, his integrity, his career, his loved ones, etc.? If so, what kind of massive misery would the Moral Establishment then be responsible for? If not, if men are actively encouraged to gain such goods, does not this utterly eviscerate the ethic of self-sacrifice?

Fourth: Now it is possible to discern the unconditional inhumanity of equating goodwill with self-sacrifice. For where is the goodwill toward the luckless individual exhorted to sacrifice himself? Where, for example, is the kindness toward the young man called upon to sacrifice his relationship with the woman he loves in order to please his family? And where the compassion for an individual who might lose years and, perhaps, life itself when drafted into the military on the grounds that he must sacrifice for his country? Where is the goodwill toward any innocent human being required to surrender any cherished value—love, freedom, hard-earned wealth, or any other—because it is his moral obligation to serve others? The logical conclusion is: there is an utter dearth of goodwill in such cases.

To "selflessly serve others"—the phrase is revealing. Notice that the abrogation of egoism diminishes some men relative to others. Because if a person is not permitted to pursue his own happiness—if some individual or society or the state has the legitimate authority to demand of him a sacrifice of his interest—then he is of lesser value or importance than those to whom his aspirations are subordinated. He is a pawn, a mere means to their ends, a peon to be deployed as fodder to their aristocratic purposes.

Fifth: Ayn Rand identified the logical contradiction inherent in a self-sacrifice ethic. The beneficiary of a good deed accepts the kindness offered—on what terms and for which reason? Because, in some form, it benefits him. He receives it, in other words, on egoistic motives. But if egoism is morally wrong, then how can the provider of the service be party to such a transgression? And how can his virtue be intimately interwoven with another's vice?

None of this makes sense. Only if egoism is a proper code is there moral probity in the recipient's selfish acceptance of the good turn done him—and in the benefactor's caring provision.

Sixth: How then is goodwill to be promoted among mankind? Human beings differ on many important issues, including regarding moral principles, but the best among them agree on a salient point: human life is precious. How, then, to stimulate among the vast majority of the human race an active caring for their fellow man?

By teaching each individual that his life belongs to him—that he should fulfill his values and be joyously happy—that he has no duty to others beyond respecting their right to do the same—and that he should actively help another man only if he wants to.

In reality, other human beings—and respectful relations with them—represent an enormous value to a rational man. In them, he finds love, family, friendship, and education, not to mention a division of labor economy, in which he need not grow his own food or create other necessities but can specialize in the field he loves, earn money, and trade peacefully with other productive men in satisfaction of his needs. If others are not gangsters, dictators, or plunderers—if they respect his right to his own life—the prospective benefits of friendly relations are too varied to enumerate.

What factor, then, prevents many from apprehending what seems an obvious truth?

The key to the question's answer lies in the phrase, "if they respect his right to his own life." *But what if they do not?*

What if they claim that he lacks a right to his own life—that he must sacrifice for others—and that he is "selfish" and immoral if he elects not to?

Then they teach him that other persons are his enemy and that he must make an inhuman choice: happiness or morality. He can achieve values and be happy—but "selfish" and immoral; or he can surrender values to others and be unhappy but self-denyingly virtuous.

An individual will not feel love or affection toward one for whom he must sacrifice. He will experience only frustration, resentment, and bitterness. For example, if parents demand a child give up career choice for one favored by the family, the child's accession does not enhance but undermines his family intimacy. The sacrifice leads ineluctably to less affection for the parents—not more.

On the other hand, if we teach our children—and others—that the proper course of action is value achievement, self-fulfillment, and joyous life, we thereby show men that other human beings are no danger to their values or happiness. We remove the threat of deprivation that a self-sacrifice code dangles above their heads like the Sword of Damocles.

In positive terms and above all: we show a man that other human beings stand in support of his quest for values.

An authentic kindness toward one's brothers and sisters requires, as a baseline starting point, a sincere recognition of their need and right to pursue values—and a definitive refusal to call upon them to sacrifice those values.

Genuine benevolence toward another person necessitates undying support for that person's effort to gain values.

Certainly, in some terms, this truth is recognized by mankind's most conscientious parents—and their children grow up to experience not a dutiful but a loving bond with those parents.

When an ethos of unflinching value support is persistently conveyed—or, at the very least, when exhortations of value sacrifice are not routinely imposed—an individual's characteristic attitude toward others will manifest immeasurably more sincere generosity than in the reverse case.

Truth is often paradoxical. Few in the modern world before Copernicus believed the non-obvious claim that the earth revolved around the sun—for the sun is observed to move across the sky. Fewer before Newton conceived that the force causing a coin dropped from the hand to plummet to earth was the identical power constraining the planets in their orbits, preventing them hurtling into space—because the scale of the contrasting events was of such immensely differing magnitudes. Perhaps none before Pasteur thought that seemingly puny microbes could engender lethal disease in organisms millions of times larger. Certainly none before Rand understood that kindly goodwill could be promoted by encouraging selfishness, and only in this fashion. Yet all of these principles are true.

Egoism and the authentic benevolence to which it inevitably leads—applied to politics—are integrated into capitalism's essence and constitute a significant part of its matchless moral rectitude.

Chapter Seven
Capitalism as the Sole System of Moral Virtue

Capitalism is the system of prodigious value creation. Its production of immense material wealth and a consequent rise of real income across all social strata have previously been discussed. The flowering of literature in the free nations, the publishing of original books on every topic from anthropology to zoology, the composition and recording of every conceivable form of music from opera to rap and rock, the flourishing of philosophy departments in a thousand universities—all of the varied forms of intellectual/spiritual wealth created under capitalism—has been merely touched upon, but is evident to even causal observation of culture in the Free World.

Every aspect of man's existence—from sheer physical survival, to flourishing material affluence, to intellectual-cultural fulfillment—human life in every form, covering thousands of varied instances—relies upon the creation of values.

The measure of a social system's moral worth is its ability—or lack thereof—to promote the creation of values. The system of individual rights stands supremely, superlatively alone in this all-important regard. Why?

The answer involves two central, inter-related points: egoism and rationality.

An individual's right to create and dispose of values must be protected by law. This is the liberating, life-giving function served by the principle of individual rights. *Individual rights protects a man's freedom to live and act egoistically.* Under its legal rubric, he is free to create values, to dispose of them as he will, and to seek his own happiness. *The principle of inalienable individual rights legally unleashes all of the creative powers latent in men's need to attain values.*

Individual rights are the logical application of an egoistic, value-driven moral code to political philosophy and practice.

By contrast, under socialism—or statism in any of its myriad iterations—moral rectitude resides pre-eminently in selfless service to the state; egoism is expunged, often ruthlessly; and men are prohibited—in full or in part—from pursuing values. Mixed economy welfare states are a mixture of value achievement and value sacrifice; totalitarian states—well-named—embody total sacrifice.

Further, in liberating men to seek survival, the selfsame principle liberates them to deploy their survival instrument in support of that quest. They are free to fully engage their minds in the mission to create values.

The results, in action, of rational egoism operating under conditions of political-economic freedom have been briefly described in this book. To conclude that they have been spectacularly life-giving—especially in stark contrast to the encompassing brutality and destitution of the pre-and-non capitalist systems—is a tepid understatement.

Individual rights are a non-negotiable social necessity of value achievement—and consequently of human life. Because capitalism is the sole system to uphold and protect them—it is the sole system superlatively able to promote life.

It is not a historic accident that living standards and expectancy of life rose dramatically—in the brief span of two centuries—in the nations in which individual rights gained currency. Capitalism, in Ayn Rand's terms, is the sole social system fully congruent with human nature and the requirements of man's survival. Capitalism, in short, is the system of life—the system of human life—the system necessary to advance the life of a rational animal.

Virtue is to choose actions that support life—capitalism is the sole system to protect and reward men's right to life-promoting choices—therefore, capitalism is the system of moral virtue.

It has been shown that egoism, properly conceived, is the necessary moral foundation to foster human kindness. Observe one specific consequence of such a broad truth: the unprecedented flowering of voluntary charity in the United States, history's most capitalistic nation.

How is such charity manifested? In 2005, for example, private philanthropy as a percentage of gross domestic product (GDP) showed the United States at the top of the list with a figure of 1.67%, more than double the percentage of the second-place nation—Great Britain. In plain terms, this means that private citizens in America gave to charity more than twice the amount of money measured in terms of percentage of income than did any other private citizenry in the world.

American citizens, for example, donated $1.78 billion in aid for relief of a devastating tsunami in south Asia and $78 million in aid when a terrible earthquake struck Pakistan. The charity organization, AmeriCares, which receives philanthropic donations from individual American citizens and from U.S. corporations, since its 1982 founding, has provided an estimated $3.4 billion of aid in over 137 countries. Beyond this, such organizations as the

American Red Cross, Habitat for Humanity, the American Cancer Society, and numerous others flourish in the United States.

Perhaps most startling when viewed in the full context of history was the billions of dollars spent by the United States to re-construct Germany and Japan after World War II. Is there another instance in world history when a victorious nation spent a vast fortune to re-build defeated enemies that had attacked it? This author knows of none. These events inspired a comic novel and subsequent movie entitled *The Mouse That Roared*, in which a backward, bankrupt nation plans to invade the United States, in the expectation of crushing defeat and ensuing American largesse.

One reason of such generosity is that the colossal creation of life-giving wealth in America *is itself a superbly beneficent phenomenon*—and, as one consequence, gives hard-working Americans the economic means of philanthropy.

But the deeper and neglected causal factor is that the egoist code, integrated into the very essence of capitalism, has morally empowered Americans to be the most magnanimous, generous people of history.

Capitalism's critics oppose it primarily on moral, not economic grounds; on the basis of a profoundly mistaken self-sacrifice code, inevitably blinding them to capitalism's myriad, manifest virtues. The major battle for capitalism is, has always been, and will remain one of fundamental moral principles.

Nevertheless, the economic case for capitalism could not be stronger, especially today; and that argument—which must necessarily be re-made for each generation, lest we forget the practical benefits of freedom—composes this slender volume's concluding section.

PART THREE
THE ECONOMIC SUPERIORITY OF CAPITALISM

Chapter Eight
The Failure of Socialism

The dictionary defines "socialism" as: "a theory or system of social organization that advocates the vesting of the ownership and control of the means of production and distribution, of capital, land, etc., in the community as a whole."

Jettison the pleasant euphemism, "community as a whole," replaced by the harsh truth, "the government"—and socialism is revealed as: the political-economic system that entails governmental ownership and control of an entire economy. (This is contrasted with mixed economies—partly socialist, partly capitalist—which will be critiqued in the next chapter.) This means that every facet of the economic system is commanded by the agency that holds a legal monopoly on the use of force in that society.

Such a system ineluctably devolves into a totalitarian state.

Observe that under full socialism, with its utter dearth of private ownership and profit seeking, there is but one producer of goods and services—the state; there is one distributor of such goods—the state; there is one employer—the state; there is one educator—the state; there is one publisher—the state; there is one builder of housing—the state; there is one grower and distributor of food—the state; there is one manufacturer and distributor of clothing—the state; and there is one provider of medical care—the state.

It is rational to conclude there will likewise be but one administrator of slave labor camps—the state.

What are the reasons that full socialism—total governmental control of the economic system—necessitates totalitarianism—total governmental control of every aspect of human life, and the systematic extirpation of freedom?

Consider: what if an individual desired to start his own business, or own his own farm, or build and possess his own home—what happens to such men? What if an intellectual strongly disagreed with governmental principles and policies? What if he desired to found his own newspaper or publishing house, and publish the works of dissenters? Would he be allowed to? Could he write for the state publisher? Would the authorities deem him insane—and mandate psychiatry, all practitioners of whom work for the state? What if the best and the brightest bristle under such repression and attempt to emigrate to freer lands—examples of the much-publicized "Brain Drain"—will they be freely permitted to exit? What happens to the socialist state when they depart?

The inevitability of totalitarianism lies in the ubiquitous abrogation of individual rights embodied in full socialism.

In reality, a government has no moral right to coercively prevent a man from starting a business, owning a farm, building a home, founding a newspaper, establishing a publishing house, or performing any of a thousand other productive activities. It is the inalienable right of a human being to pursue any life-giving value he desires—the state has no moral say in the matter.

With the principle of individual rights already disavowed, no moral law constrains the government from exacerbating its domestic repression. A government that of its very nature massively initiates coercion against its own innocent citizens will not blanch at the intensified initiation of coercion necessary to enforce its edicts.

Recalcitrant egoists, unswervingly seeking private businesses, farms, homes, newspapers, publishing houses, etc., will be remorselessly quashed by the state.

Leon Trotsky, as co-founder-and-dictator of the Soviet Union, had on his hands the blood of countless millions of innocent victims, but nevertheless provided mankind a legitimate benefit by refusing to conceal socialism's true character. He said: "In a country where the sole employer is the State, opposition means death by slow starvation. The old proverb: who does not work, shall not eat, has been replaced by a new one: *who does not obey* shall not eat." (Emphasis added.)

Full socialism is necessarily a totalitarian system and has been widely implemented—in the former Soviet Union, in China, in North Korea, in Cuba, and elsewhere. Full socialism wrought a seismically spectacular moral holocaust, leading to the extermination of fully 100 million innocent souls deemed "enemies of the state." But what have been its economic consequences?

An unmitigated disaster. The millions left unmurdered by the socialists were condemned to unrelieved destitution.

Take the Soviet Union as a leading example. Philosopher Tara Smith informs us: In the 1980s, after 70 years of socialism, "only a third of households had hot running water. As late as 1989, meat and sugar were still rationed—in peacetime…[and] an average welfare mother in the United States received more income in a month than the average Soviet worker earned in a year." Shortages were rampant; at various times, it was impossible to find dish soap, toothpaste, vacuum cleaners, or myriad other commodities—and shoes were notoriously difficult to obtain at all times. Despite untold wealth of natural resources—and massive aid from Western nations—the Soviet economy sputtered and spluttered its way across seven wheezing decades to final, abysmal collapse.

How massive was Western aid? After Lenin's socialist principles bankrupted the Russian economy, he instituted his New Economic Policy (NEP) in 1921. This involved a temporary repeal of certain controls, permitting once again private, profit-seeking ownership of small manufacturing, retailing, and wholesaling companies. (The Communists did, however, retain control of what Lenin termed "the commanding heights" of the economy, including heavy industry, mining, transportation, and foreign trade.) Regarding the failed socialist methods, Lenin remarked: "Our program was right in theory, but impractible."

So he turned to Western capitalism for salvation. He offered Western firms generous "concessions" in return for the rapid industrialization of the Soviet economy. English, German, Italian, Swedish, Danish, and American companies accepted, and scurried to provide the USSR with airfields and railroads—with gold, copper, and iron mines—with oil refineries—and much more.

But before Western industry could rebuild the shattered Soviet economy, lethal famine swept the country, impelling the West to organize massive relief efforts. The figures for the full Western aid are lost, but it is known that America alone donated 700,000 tons of foodstuff.

The brilliant German aeronautical engineer, Hugo Junkers, designed airplanes and factories for the Soviets; the English firm, Lena Goldfields Ltd., created a state-of-the-art gold-mining installation near Vitimsk; German, English, Italian, Swedish, and Norwegian companies, among others, contributed to productivity in countless fields, including agriculture, manufacture of machine tools, and construction of whaling vessels.

But the Americans were primarily responsible for industrializing the Soviet Union—to whatever degree this occurred. Examples abound: the Ford Motor Company supplied the Soviets with designs and blueprints of its models; they sent supervisory engineers to Russia; and trained Soviet personnel at the Ford plant in Dearborn, Michigan. Related: the Austin Company of New York and Ohio built the enormous factories necessary for the Ford project at Gorki.

The Cleveland firm of Arthur Mackee supplied the equipment and expertise to build huge steel plants at Magnitogorsk. During the course of this project, the Americans dammed the Ural River, constructed blast furnaces, provided training courses, and sent to America for advanced schooling the most promising Soviet workers.

The superb engineer, John Calder of Detroit, helped build and equip tractor plants first at Stalingrad, then at Chelyabinsk. Calder and his American staff erected a modern factory at Stalingrad capable of manufacturing 50,000 tractors per year, seeking to feed a country blessed with fertile farmlands but afflicted with backward agriculture.

But the crowning achievement of American capitalism transpired during Stalin's first Five Year Plan: the construction of the giant hydro-electric facility at Dnieprostroi. The dam and power station at Dnieprostroi—the world's largest—became the showpiece of Soviet propaganda, intended to establish the superiority of socialism. Its size was colossal, its construction time record-breaking, its productive capacity vast. All of these facts the Soviets broadcasted. There was only one they neglected to mention: It was built by the Americans.

Colonel Hugh Cooper, creator of the mighty Wilson Dam at Muscle Shoals, Tennessee, designed a dam over a mile in length and 200 feet in height to block the Dnieper. When completed, Cooper's plant generated 2,500,000 kilowatts of power, dwarfing his own Wilson Dam, which put out 456,320 kilowatts. Dniepostroi increased fivefold the electrical power output of the Soviet Union.

There is a deal more—indeed, Stalin himself acknowledged to American visitor, Eric Johnston, that "about two-thirds of all the large industrial enterprises in the USSR had been built with U.S. material or technical assistance"—but these examples will suffice.

How did the Soviet Union pay for all of this? The Communists looted and sold great art works to foreign museums—and stripped the Orthodox churches of their historic treasures (murdering thousands of priests, monks, and nuns in the process). The GPU—the secret police—tortured any Russian suspected of owning valuables. People with relatives in the U.S. were forced to write letters begging for dollars, which, upon arrival, were seized by the state. As part of their unremitting class war, they executed millions for the crime of being "bourgeois," and stole every item of property to the last penny.

Further, under both Lenin and Stalin, the Soviet regime infamously followed a "Starve, but export" policy: it shipped grain from the Ukrainian "black earth" country—the world's most fertile grain-producing soil—abroad, and permitted millions of Russians to die of famine. Nicolas Werth, in the profoundly important, *The Black Book of Communism*, informs us: "Despite the massive international relief effort, at least 5 million...Russians...died of hunger in 1921 and 1922." Often the government simply broke contracts and did not pay their benefactors at all.

In keeping with this last was America's Lend-Lease program of World War II. German historian, Werner Keller, writes that under this policy, "the immense industrial potential of the United States was put freely at the disposal of the Soviet Union." During the war, a staggering amount of goods was shipped or flown to Soviet Russia: raw materials, manufacturing plants, tools, machinery, spare parts, clothing, textiles, canned food, flour, in addition to a vast supply of armaments.

Lend-Lease was arranged as an interest free loan. Not a penny was repaid. It ended up a gift from capitalism to socialism—a gift worth 10,800,000,000— indeed, a much vaster sum considering the greater value of 1940s' dollars. President Roosevelt, who once stated that "Stalin is not an imperialist," openly believed in giving to the Soviet dictator everything he could while seeking nothing in return.

This explains American laxity enabling Soviet agents to engage in massive looting in America. Both Keller and British historian, Antony Sutton, document that during World War II and the years following, the U.S. was a haven for Soviet spies. The Roosevelt administration trusted its Soviet allies, and permitted Russian Lend-Lease agents virtually unlimited access to witness and/or study U.S. inventions and industrial secrets. Soviet spies memorized, copied, and/or stole plans of American products and industrial methods. The Soviets pilfered in enormous quantities: blueprints, inventions, machinery, and such classified materials as uranium and heavy water. The Communist agents packed them into huge crates marked "diplomatic mail," and shipped them from the U.S. airbase at Great Falls, Montana, a principal link in the American airlift to Russia. The U.S. military provided the planes in which their Soviet "allies" shipped the stolen goods to Russia.

Examination of recently-opened Soviet archives and the 1995 de-classification of the top secret Venona Project—the World War II enterprise in which American cryptographers cracked the Soviet code—validated with full certainty the shocking truth: the Roosevelt and Truman administrations were rife with Stalin's agents. Harry Dexter White, Assistant Secretary of the Treasury Department, was a Soviet agent. Alger Hiss, a top-ranking official at the State department and a trusted advisor to President Roosevelt at Yalta, was a Soviet agent. Lauchlin Currie, senior administrative assistant to President Roosevelt, was a Soviet agent. There were hundreds of others, including many not working directly for the U.S. government.

Espionage against the United States engaged in by American Communists resulted in the pilferage of vital American military and industrial secrets, leading to the immense strengthening of the Soviet Union. This included, of course, the infamous theft of information by Julius and Ethel Rosenberg that led to a Soviet atomic bomb. The Soviets, though not very good at science, technology, or industry, were expert at spying and stealing.

That Communism is as evil a system as National Socialism is clear—but not the point in this context. The fundamental issue here is: Communist economic development relied to a staggering degree on the achievements of Western capitalism. It was the private companies of the United States and other free nations that enabled Soviet Russia to reach whatever degree of industrialization it attained. That subsequent Cold War relations between capitalist America and socialist Russia was adversarial is not to be doubted; but what is revealing, although not surprising, is the degree to which their nexus was not one of conflict—but of abject dependency.

In Cuba conditions were hardly better. Tens of thousands of dissenters were shot—concentration camps coercing political prisoners to slave labor persist—borders, of course, are closed—and attempted escapees killed.

The economic results of such repression are predictable. Food is perpetually rationed. It is common for eggs to be doled out fourteen per family per month—when eggs are plentiful; two bars of soap per family per month—some months; and no meat. The nation's vaunted medical system is a shambles, for there is chronic shortage of even rudimentary supplies. Forget MRI machines—the system lacks basic medicines. Miguel Faria, a physician and Cuban defector, writes: "Much of what doctors are prescribing for their patients in Cuba today, if available at all, is being sent from Miami to those souls who are fortunate enough to have relatives in the U.S." The hospitals lack soap, clean linen and towels, in addition to medications, and patients must bring their own. Regarding technology—with a total of 229,000 telephones for a population of 11 million, Cuba possesses one of the world's least developed telephone systems.

Today, a common apology blames Cuba's abysmal poverty on the United States, specifically on the American trade embargo. But the embargo was always more political posturing than reality; for one thing, the Americans propped up the Soviet Union, who propped up Cuba; for another, both countries permit remittances from Cuban-Americans, whom Castro, in desperation, began referring to as "economic immigrants" rather than as "traitors."

More fundamentally, such an apology concedes the main economic point—for Marx and his heirs claimed socialism would out produce capitalism, but contemporary socialists whine that without trade and/or aid from capitalist nations the socialist countries subsist in wretched poverty. The new mantra reduces to the plea that socialism be permitted to exist parasitically off of capitalism in yet another form.

Regarding North Korea, the globe's most consistently socialist system, it might be rational to conclude "the less said the better," except that mankind must know what socialism entails for its luckless citizenry. Such knowledge may prevent other peoples from sharing the North Koreans' fate, and, in time, might assist the demise of that Stalinist regime.

Communist North Korea has the misfortune to be the most brutally repressive dictatorship on earth. Every aspect of human life—not just economic—has been nationalized; there exist no individuals, merely ciphers; no entities, only non-entities to be disposed of by the state, which executes, tortures, and enslaves innocent men with no greater remorse than stomping a beetle. "All of North Korea is a gulag," a senior U.S. official told NBC News—but, for some, conditions are more hideous than for others. Hundreds of thousands of innocents—men, women, and young children—toil in the regime's slave labor camps, some of whose conditions are sufficiently inhumane to expunge, annually, twenty to twenty-five percent of the camp's populace.

The magnitude of repression and terror is unimaginable in the West—and, not to make light of such horror, makes the former Soviet Union appear like Disneyland by comparison.

The economic results? America and other nations supplied prodigious quantities of food—an amount yet insufficient to maintain the lives of 2 million human beings dead there of starvation.

When minimal capitalist aid is forthcoming, socialist regimes collapse immediately to pre-industrial living standards; with maximal aid, it takes decades.

What are the fundamental reasons of socialism's inability to create even bare subsistence?

THE SYSTEM OF RATIONAL PLANNING

Socialist intellectuals have long advertised the system as "a planned economy," because a central governmental agency maps out every aspect of production and distribution and is, therefore, able to achieve an "integrated" allocation of resources. For example, central planners have information regarding available leather, rubber, and canvas; they know factory capacities and production schedules; they are aware of society's population, gender breakdown, age classifications, and clothing requirements.

They are, consequently, able to harmonize resources with human need and manufacture just the quantity of shoes—neither more nor less—that society requires. No underproduction—and barefoot citizens; no overproduction—and precious resources subtracted from manufacture of other vital goods.

According to these same theorists, such productive concordance is unachievable under capitalism. Because it lacks a central planning authority, each businessman plans his own output, uncoordinated with that of any other. He knows and/or controls only his own firm's raw materials, production schedule, customer preferences—not that of his rivals—resulting in a competition for remunerative markets, and an under-serving of those less lucrative, a "chaos of production" that may benefit wealthy businesses and their affluent clientele but not society in full.

Central planners formulate a comprehensive vision—to benefit society. Private businessmen devise a narrow scheme—to benefit their company. Governmental planners soar to heights effectuating spacious vistas, while private businessmen wriggle in the mud; grand-scale planners gain an eagle's eye perspective of an economy; private businessmen suffer from a worm's eye view. Socialist theory offers a pleasant vision of broad-based knowledge and centrally planned prosperity.

Reality shatters delusions.

In the real world, shoes of every size, style, and color are plentiful under capitalism; virtually impossible to procure under socialism. In actual practice, capitalism is a cornucopia—a horn of abundance—of every conceivable commodity; socialism, a horn of meagerness—shortly, a horn of famine—inevitably, a broken horn.

What is the fundamental economic error of socialist theory?

Rational planning is absolutely necessary to an economy's success. *But it is possible only under capitalism—definitively unachievable under socialism.*

In a capitalist system, economic planning takes place every day, all day, in spectacularly diverse forms. It occurs when a businessman plans to expand his productive capacity—to contract it—or to rest content; when he plans to hire additional employees—or lay off members of his existing work force; when he plans to move his plant—or remain at its present locale. Rational planning takes place when an individual devises a budget, calculates expenses, plans savings and investments—even when he chooses to buy a new coat or go one last winter with an old one. Planning occurs when a worker decides to seek new employment or retain his present one; when he chooses to relocate or remain in his current precinct; when he plans to upgrade his skills or stand pat on those he has.

Planning occurs, in a free country, on every minute occasion that an individual calculates any aspect of his economic existence—his career or job, his savings or investments, his residence, his expenditures, his business, etc. Human beings engage in rational planning on every occasion—without exception—that they cogitate regarding actions serving their interests as either sellers or buyers.

"Planning" in this context means rational thought regarding the achievement of economic values. Capitalism enjoys immense, insuperable advantages over socialism in this regard.

First: In sheer quantity of deployed mind power, socialism limits planning to a few (or few thousand) economists/bureaucrats in the Board of Economic Planners; every one else is planned for; several thousand "planners" plan for tens of millions; the tens of millions—including doctors, researchers, lawyers, farmers, workers, potential entrepreneurs, et. al., with all of their acquired knowledge and specialized expertise—are excluded from the planning process, their minds compelled to lie inoperatively dormant regarding the economic realm.

But capitalism unleashes all of this latently productive brain power; it liberates untold quantities of human intelligence to plan the achievement of economic values. *Twenty million minds now focus on the problems of economic production—not twenty thousand.* Creativity is thereby maximized; new ideas flourish; inventiveness and originality are promoted; mankind advances.

Eminent American economist, Julian Simon, argues famously that human intelligence—not iron, coal, or fertile lands, etc.—is "the ultimate resource" and that population growth, far from being a problem, is a boon, for it increases the number of rational minds to resolve the dilemmas of human existence. "We see the resource system as being as unlimited as the number of thoughts a person might have."

Second: A related point is that capitalism immeasurably surpasses socialism not merely in the quantity of minds engaged in economic planning—but in the quality of those minds. Full socialism is a totalitarian system, as noted. Its political leaders inevitably are such men as Stalin, Mao, and Castro. *The nature of the system attracts to leadership those who seek maximum power, not maximum production.* Active minds are a threat to these men and are recognized as such; in myriad forms, they are censored, silenced, suppressed—and the economy collapses or never rises to an elevation rendering collapse possible.

Under capitalism, however, neither Edison nor Bell nor the Wright brothers nor Carver nor Carnegie, et. al., need permission from the political authorities or the Central Planning Board to engage in creative thought; they plan the allocation of their own time and resources—and are free to reach out to potential backers, investors, and customers, who independently plan the disposal of their financial assets.

The bitter truth is that under socialism planning is conducted by statist politicians and their bureaucratic appointees, i.e., by power seekers and their flunkies, not by inventors, innovators, and entrepreneurs, i.e., men of productive ability. Economically, socialism versus capitalism reduces to the Stalins and Castros versus the Edisons and Carnegies. Regarding planning and production, this is no contest.

Third: The purpose of production is consumption—to deploy values, to enjoy life. Who knows best which specific values will engender individual fulfillment—an individual himself or the Central Planners? Can twenty million individuals, each judging for himself, best discern his own values and plan accordingly? Or can Central Planners in the nation's capital—that do not and could not possibly know a fraction of the citizens and their aspirations—most fruitfully plan out their economic lives? An exact formulation of the question renders evident its own response.

Values are personal—the meaning of each man's life—and their maximal achievement necessitates individual freedom to think, to plan, and to act in their pursuit.

Fourth: the price system exists only in a capitalist system, not in a socialist one; its presence expedites economic planning, its absence eradicates it. The price system of a free market, and the critical task it performs in economic calculation, is a complex issue, largely beyond the scope of this book. Here, one aspect can be focused on: its role in facilitating value achievement.

Reduce the issue to its simplest terms. For example, prices indicate, among other points, consumer demand for a product. Customers display value preferences in the marketplace daily by their willingness to expend more of their income for one commodity over another. The greater demand for X over Y, reflected in its higher price, tells producers that—other matters being equal—the manufacture of X is more lucrative than the manufacture of Y. In pursuit of maximal profit they then proceed to expand production of X—and customers benefit from an increased supply of a valued commodity.

By contrast, how would central governmental planners know which commodity is most valued by millions of customers? In the absence of a free marketplace swarming with millions of buyers and sellers, whose self-interested preferences are ceaselessly reflected in prices, how could central planners know the shifting, swirling value predilections of numberless individuals?

The concise, simple, brutally accurate answer is: they could not.

Granted, it requires an enormous stretch of imagination to believe that socialist dictators care about the value fulfillment and personal happiness of individual citizens. But if, in some fantastic thought experiment it could be conceived that a benign individual held absolute sway—rather than a mass murderer—how could he and his economic advisors gain the specific information necessary to facilitate the value attainment of his subjects?

By extirpating the Central Planning Board, liberating the marketplace, and thereby empowering millions to plan for themselves.

That rational planning is possible only under capitalism, unachievable under full socialism, is a specific economic instance of two broader, related philosophic principles: the mind is man's instrument of survival—and the mind's full functioning entails recognition of individual rights.

But the mixed economy welfare states of the modern Western world are neither fully socialist nor fully capitalist. How is their economic performance assessed—when contrasted with a system of fully-protected individual rights?

Chapter Nine
The Failure of a Mixed Economy

A mixed economy combines capitalist elements with socialist ones; meaning it combines protection of individual rights with abrogation of them. The examination of the Inventive Period showed the results of virtually unfettered capitalism; the analysis of full socialism displayed its results. A mixed economy is a farrago of clashing elements—the component of freedom leading to prosperity, the statist element curtailing it.

Every ill of a mixed economy—monopolies, inflation, depression, etc.—are caused by the statist element of the mixture, and are impossible under laissez-faire. They can be examined one at a time.

COERCIVE MONOPOLIES

Anti-capitalist intellectuals claim that on a free market, unregulated by government, ruthless entrepreneurs carve out vast empires, suppress competition, and charge arbitrarily high prices. The truth, however, is that this claim is historically inaccurate and economically invalid; indeed, exactly reversed: such monopolies result solely from government's regulation of the market, and are impossible in its absence.

Take as a prime example the notorious Central Pacific Railroad, which virtually controlled California for the better part of three decades—the rapacious "Octopus" of Frank Norris' famous novel. This railroad, built and operated by the "Big Four" of Leland Stanford, Collis Huntington, Charles Crocker, and Mark Hopkins, was guilty of every abusive practice of which monopolies are popularly accused. Its leaders bribed state legislators, suppressed competition, and charged ruinous rates. From the mid-1870s until the turn of the 20th century, its insatiable appetite gobbled huge percentages of profits reaped by California producers. How did the railroad attain the power to perpetrate such unscrupulous practices?

By the power of government backing.

The California state legislature granted the railroad a legal monopoly in the state, coercively debarring competitors entering the field. For example, the legislature bestowed on the road control of the coastal areas surrounding San Francisco Bay, prohibiting other railroads access to the port. During the 30-year period of the Central Pacific's hegemony, legislative action defeated several attempts by private businessmen to open competing lines.

None of the abuses could have occurred in the absence of legal monopoly status granted by the state. The state's control of the railroad industry was the decisive factor responsible for the injustices. Ayn Rand reminds us: "What made this possible? It was done through the power of the California legislature. The Big Four controlled the legislature and held the state closed to competitors by legal restrictions..." Burton Folsom provides further details: "Stanford, who was elected Governor and U.S. Senator, controlled politics for the Big Four and prevented any competing railroad from entering California."

If governmental bodies are constitutionally debarred from economic intervention, if they are relegated by law solely to the protection of individual rights—emphatically including the prohibition and punishment of all instances of initiating force or fraud—then corrupt businessmen could not buy political favors, and could not legally prevent honest rivals from entering their respective fields.

It has been pointed out both by capitalism's critics and its supporters that government regulatory bodies often fall under control of the businesses they ostensibly regulate—to the detriment of competition. Indeed, the power to legally suppress competition is the reason that big businesses often politically support regulation and the legislation that spawns it.

The confused logic of a mixed economy inevitably favors already successful, entrenched companies at the expense of start-up firms. Theoretically, regulatory agencies are established to serve the "public good"—however such a malleably elastic term is defined. In countless ways a successful company claims to serve said "public good." Company executives point out that their firm employs thousands of workers, serves millions of customers, etc., and has done so for decades. Further, the established companies contribute to many worthy causes (including campaign contributions to the elected officials who appoint the regulators). Consequently, to curtail the company's business is to undermine the very "public good" the bureaucrats seek to preserve.

In the nature of things, entrepreneurial firms, just starting up, have yet to gain millions of customers, hire thousands of workers, amass sufficient fortunes to donate fulsomely to charity (or to powerful politicians), etc. They are inherently at a disadvantage negotiating with regulators and influencing governmental policy.

Under laissez-faire, innovative entrepreneurs have only to convince the customers that they have a superior product—and though that generally takes time, they have often succeeded in doing so. But if the economy is controlled, the entrenched canal interests, for example, can convince the regulators to grant them monopoly status in the shipping industry, legally banning the germinating railroads. The gas light companies can do the same, resulting in a legal prohibition on the nascent electric light. The carriage makers and blacksmiths can promote an identical policy in the automobile's infancy, etc. The logic of regulation militates against innovation and entrepreneurship in favor of preferential legal status for already-entrenched companies who seek to avoid the necessity of competing.

If the California state government had not granted the railroad the status of legal monopoly, then other entrepreneurs could have (and would have) entered the field. The resulting competition would have prevented the Central Pacific from charging arbitrarily high rates. The open competition of a free marketplace would have avoided the detriment to farmers and shippers. Government regulation was not the remedy to the abuses of the Big Four; it was the enabling cause. Laissez-faire was not the problem; it was the liberating solution.

This point was illustrated when Edward H. Harriman took over the Union Pacific, the Central Pacific's "Siamese twin," which, built with federal subsidies and land grants, suffered from sloppy construction and corrupt management, lapsing inevitably into bankruptcy. Harriman thoroughly renovated the line, and, in the absence of legal monopoly status, had no choice but to compete. With no power to charge arbitrarily high prices, Harriman did what a great businessman functioning in a competitive marketplace does: he managed his operation with matchless efficiency. Within a decade he doubled the tonnage of freight shipped per mile of his track—and he slashed freight rates by from fifteen to seventeen percent. He amassed a fortune by prodigiously productive effort, not by invoking governmental coercion.

Those readers familiar with *Atlas Shrugged* recognize the predatory mixed economy businessmen—James Taggart and Orren Boyle in the novel—who seek profit not via productivity in a competitive marketplace, but by currying favor with powerful politicos who pass laws to suppress competitors. Francis Ford Coppola's 1988 film, *Tucker*, loosely based on the life of American automotive entrepreneur, Preston Tucker, also provides a vividly artistic example. In the story, Tucker's innovations were financially threatening to entrenched Detroit auto makers, who lobbied a powerful Michigan Senator to introduce restrictive legislation.

In real life, a coercive monopoly is one that can charge virtually any price it pleases without regard for the interest or appraisal of its customers. Business economist, Alan Greenspan, in the years before he became Federal Reserve Chairman, defined such a monopoly as "a business concern that can set its prices and production policies independent of the market, with immunity from competition, from the law of supply and demand." No company on a free market can do this. Under capitalism, every company, despite its wealth or popularity, must compete in the marketplace with numberless rivals.

In a free society, a company competes both with contestants in its field—and with firms manufacturing a commodity substitutable for its product. The Coca-Cola Company, for example, popular and wealthy as it is, must compete daily not merely with Pepsi and RC Cola, but with dozens of diverse soft drinks—varied soda flavors, iced tea, iced coffee, lemonade, carbonated water, etc—that serve as viable alternatives. Thirsty customers, seeking a non-alcoholic beverage, encounter myriad choices. Daily, Coca-Cola must win new customers and win anew prior ones. The sole means to accomplish this is to provide customers affordable products they prefer.

Open competition on a free market precludes the possibility of such coercive monopolies as the Central Pacific Railroad.

Greenspan again: "The necessary precondition of a coercive monopoly is closed entry—the barring of all competing producers from a given field. This can be accomplished only by an act of government intervention, in the form of special regulations, subsidies or franchise."

Unfortunately, many capitalists seek government intervention as means of legally suppressing competition—thereby undercutting capitalism. This is a manifestation of a mixed economy—one sufficiently free for private business to exist, but sufficiently unfree to admit governmentally initiated coercion—and would be properly obviated by a policy of laissez-faire.

When legislation is passed that does not coercively restrain criminals, then it coerces honest men. If laws do not punish initiation of force or fraud, then they punish legitimate—often productive—human activities. If laws serve no rational function, they serve an irrational one.

Any and all instances of initiating force or fraud by businessmen can and must be prohibited by law and punished severely by the criminal justice system. But it is manifestly unjust and economically bootless to legally curtail the productive activities of honest men. Beyond the indispensably vital protection of individual rights provided by the criminal and civil justice system, the government has no role to play in an economy.

The rational and moral solution to coercive monopolies is a constitutional amendment prohibiting government from regulating business.

COERCIVE UNIONISM — AND UNEMPLOYMENT

The single form of coercive monopoly favored by anti-capitalists is: labor unions.

Unions seek, and through governmental coercion gain, monopolistic control over an industry's labor supply. This situation can best be comprehended by contrast with the labor market under unrestricted capitalism.

Under laissez-faire, an employer is free to hire any worker, unionized or not, willing to work at the wages and terms he proposes—and all workers, not merely those belonging to unions, are free to accept or reject his offer. Where freedom prevails, monetary wage rates are set by practice of supply and demand, by the competition among employers for workers and among workers for jobs.

But in the American mixed economy, such Congressional legislation as the National Labor Relations Act (1935) and others, and a succession of Supreme Court rulings, often compelled employers to recognize and bargain with unions—and forced non-union workers to accept the union as their sole bargaining agent.

Most important: Nobel Laureate Milton Friedman points out that law enforcement agencies and the court system often "tolerate behavior in the course of labor disputes that they would never tolerate under other circumstances." In American history, there is an endless number of cases in which union members initiated hideous violence against workers sufficiently independent to cross picket lines during strikes—"scabs" in the unions' non-objective nomenclature—and suffered little or no legal punishment for their crimes. Law professor, Sylvester Petro, reminds us that representative of such cases was the Kohler Strike in Wisconsin in 1954—in which "employees attempting to enter the plant were slugged, kneed in the groin, kicked, pushed and threatened."

Friedman states: "It is almost impossible to obtain legal protection against mass picketing, which is inherently intimidating." Nor is it uncommon during strikes for independent workers to be murdered by union violence. In one such case, of many, dozens of "scabs" were murdered by members of the striking United Mine Workers in Herrin, Illinois in 1922.

If grotesque violence during labor disputes is currently minimal, it is not because labor unions are more civilized, but because employers have ceased hiring independent workers during strikes. By a combination of government coercion and threat of union violence they have been stripped of their right to hire any worker(s) they deem satisfactory. Economist, Henry Hazlitt, explains this point brilliantly:

> Now a strike is not...merely the act of a worker in "withholding his labor," or even merely a collusion of a large group of workers simultaneously to "withhold their labor" or give up their jobs. The whole point of a strike is the insistence by the strikers that they have not given up their jobs at all. They contend that they are still employees—in fact, the only legitimate employees. They claim an ownership of the jobs at which they refuse to work; they claim the "right" to prevent anybody else from taking the jobs that they have abandoned. That is the purpose of their mass picket lines, and of the vandalism and violence that they either resort to or threaten. They insist that the employer has no right to replace them with other workers, temporary or permanent, and they mean to see to it that he doesn't. Their demands are enforced always by intimidation and coercion, and in the last resort by actual violence.

Union violence against independent workers is eminently logical given the basic intent of coercive unionization: *such workers threaten their monopolization of the labor supply*. If employers were legally free to bargain with any and all workers—as is their moral right—unions would lose their coercive advantage in negotiations.

It goes without saying that, in a free society, workers have an inalienable right to organize and present a united front to management if they so choose. But owners also possess inalienable rights. They have a right to refuse to negotiate with unions, if they choose; to negotiate separately and independently with non-union workers, if they prefer; and to hire non-union workers. Further, just as workers have a right to organize, so they possess a right of refusal: they may foreswear forming, joining, or negotiating collectively with a union, reserving their right to bargain independently with employers. Everybody's rights must be protected—not just those of unions and their memberships.

Governmentally backed unions—a product of a mixed economy—are inherently a farrago of mixed morality: part productive work force—and part criminal gang seeking to extort higher wages from the company that provides their jobs by gaining an unchallengeable, violence-threatening stranglehold on an industry's labor supply. They are unremitting monopolists.

Legislation supported by such coercive unions is responsible for significant quantities of unemployment.

Unemployment for those willing and able to work is caused by government intervention in the labor market. When the government imposes minimum wage laws, for example, or when it stipulates employer bargaining exclusively with labor unions, there follow logically two results: higher pay for those who can get jobs—and an increasing number of those who cannot.

Analyze the effects of minimum wage laws, for example. To choose an arbitrary figure, imagine the government sets the minimum wage at $6 per hour or $240.00 for a forty-hour week. One immediate consequence is that no one whose labor is worth less than $6 per hour will be employed. Henry Hazlitt makes the important point that: "You cannot make a man worth a given amount by making it illegal to offer him anything less." The minimum wage merely deprives him of the opportunity to work at a level that his current skills permit—and it deprives the firm and, ultimately, the customers of the modest output of his labor. The essence of the situation is that, for a low wage, the government has substituted unemployment.

Indeed, the situation is worse. For now unemployed, the aspiring worker is deprived not merely of a limited income but also of an opportunity to enhance work skills with which to earn higher future wages. No "on-the-job" training exists for one who holds no job.

In the name of "helping" the poor worker, minimum wage laws have the following impact on him: they deprive him of income, work experience, opportunity to demonstrate work ethic and personal responsibility, possible on-the-job training, and pride of productive effort.

Minimum wage laws discriminate against those with minimum skills, because such laws threaten to price them out of the labor market.

The effect is similar when the government capitulates to the political demands of unions. By means of government-enforced monopoly of an industry's labor supply, and/or by initiation of violence against independent workers during strikes, or threat of such violence, unions are able to compel wages above levels they would attain if labor negotiations remained fully voluntary. Such gains come principally at the expense of other workers.

Milton Friedman points out: "The key to understanding the situation is the most elementary principle of economics: the law of demand—the higher the price of anything, the less of it people will be willing to buy. Make labor of any kind more expensive and the number of jobs of that kind will be fewer." For example, the more construction workers are paid, the higher are building costs. Purchase of a home becomes correspondingly more expensive, and fewer people will buy. Consequently, fewer houses than otherwise are built and fewer workers are hired.

A union that coercively raises wages reduces the number of jobs in the field it controls. The workers unhireable at the higher wage, who would be employed at a lower one, seek elsewhere for employment, the increased supply of job hungry workers consequently driving down wage rates in other fields. Wages forced above market levels for one group inevitably reduce the wages paid to others. By the 1980s, extensive research indicated that, on average, about 10 to 15 percent of American workers had, via union power, raised their wages roughly 10 to 15 percent above market levels. Their gain had reduced the wages of the other 85 to 90 percent of workers by some 4 percent below what they otherwise might have commanded.

Moreover, all individuals, including union members, suffer in their role as customers. The point again is simple: if the teamsters' union, for example, succeeds in forcing wages above market levels, then everybody pays higher prices for goods delivered by truck, including the teamsters.

The solution is not, as some union leaders propose, to unionize all workers and proceed to force wages above free market levels universally. The necessary results of such a policy are massive unemployment, diminished productivity, and declining real wages.

Henry Hazlitt pointed out the steps that must be taken. "If employers were not legally compelled to 'bargain' with...a specified union...if employers were free to discharge strikers and peaceably to hire replacements, and if mass picketing and violence were really prohibited, the natural competitive checks on excessive wage demands would once more come into play."

The moral virtue is the legal excising of initiated violence and the maintenance of labor relations on a voluntary basis. One economic benefit is attainment of full employment; a resulting one is increased productivity and rising real income.

All that is necessary to achieve productive full employment is the operation of an unrestricted labor market in which employers and employees are free to act egoistically. If wages are free to fall to levels at which even the most unskilled worker can be productively employed, then unemployment is eradicated. This is in an employee's self-interest, as well as his employer's, because it is vastly preferable to be employed at a lower wage than unemployed at a higher one.

Anti-capitalists express universal consternation at such "a cold-hearted" proposal, drawing no distinction between monetary and real income, and gratuitously assuming that a reduction in monetary wage rates necessitates diminished workers' living standards. The exact reverse is true: expunging the union's monopolistic power will, for several reasons, raise all men's real wealth, including that of the most unskilled workers.

Recall the fundamentals: wealth is goods, not money—and is increased by one means solely: maximization of productivity.

Breaking the unions' monopolistic power, and permitting wage rates to fall to levels reached by fully voluntary negotiation, enhance productiveness in two central regards.

First: the attainment of full employment actualizes an economy's productive potential. The more men gainfully employed, the greater the creation of goods and services.

Second: it extirpates the egregiously anti-production policies of the coercive unions.

Observe the countless forms in which government-backed unions assail productivity. They support "feather-bedding" practices, in which more men than necessary must be hired for a job, thereby wasting valuable time of often skilled workers who could be productively employed on other projects. They promote rigid subdivisions of labor, in which workers qualified for a specific task will nevertheless be disqualified from its performance because it falls outside their narrow job description. Often they oppose the introduction of labor-saving machinery, thereby reducing the efficiency of labor. They discourage competition among workers that seek to increase productivity. Frequently they oppose advancement for merit, supporting instead advancement for seniority—and resist payment based on output, insisting on equal hourly rates. Nor is this all—an enumerated list of the unions' perverse war on productiveness could continue—but such examples suffice.

Eliminate such irrational depredations, liberate each worker to produce to his full capacity, and society is significantly wealthier, not poorer. The skyrocketing increase of production entails expanded supply of consumer goods and services, increased purchasing power, and rising real income. The immense step up in productiveness may or may not rival that of Britain's Industrial Revolution and America's Inventive Period—such is impossible to predict—but an immense step up it will indubitably be.

The most difficult items to discern are a system's foregone benefits—the things that do not come into existence because of it. The houses not built, the automobiles not manufactured, the roads not completed (or even begun), etc., are extremely difficult to identify, for men readily observe what is, not what is not. The wealth uncreated because monopolistic unions coercively diminish men's productivity is imperceivable, but nonetheless real, rendering all men immeasurably poorer.

Observe an important parallel. On a free market, a private company cannot gain a coercive monopoly. If the government has no power to grant preferential legal status, then a powerful company has no means to exclude rivals. The possibility and reality of competition keeps companies from imposing arbitrary prices and terms on their customers.

Similarly, on a free market, a labor union cannot gain a coercive monopoly. If the government does not abrogate the right of employers and non-union workers to negotiate independently—and if it protects their physical safety in doing so—then a powerful union has no legal means to exclude rivals. The possibility and reality of competition keep unions from imposing arbitrary wage rates and terms on their employers.

Coercive monopolies are possible only under a policy of governmental interventionism—engendered by the statist component of a mixed economy—impossible under capitalism. The supporters of laissez-faire, upholding the principle of individual rights, universally condemn all coercive monopolies. But the enemies of capitalism, essentially influenced by Marx, continue to wage a "class struggle," and profess empathy for the poor. In their view, the rights of innocent individuals can be mercilessly trampled, including those of countless workers, so long as the powerful labor unions benefit. The sole coercive monopolies they morally oppose are those supposedly bestowing advantages on corporate "fat cats." Those theoretically favoring union members are morally praiseworthy.

INFLATION

A pattern emerges from the first two examples: the economic (and moral) ills of a mixed economy proceed from the statist—not the free—element of the mixture. This pattern holds in all cases.

Many people mistakenly believe that inflation is an increase in prices of goods and services. The truth, however, is that rising prices are a consequence of inflation. Inflation itself is simply the government's expansion of the money supply. Hazlitt says: "Inflation, always and everywhere, is caused by an increase in the supply of money and credit. In fact, inflation *is* the increase in the supply of money and credit."

If benevolent men desire universal prosperity, why not simply empower the government—in the form of the Federal Reserve System—to print massive amounts of currency and distribute it to the American people, a million dollars per head (or more)? Poverty is thereby eliminated and all citizens live comfortably. Or will they?

They will not. The increase in money greatly stimulates demand without a corresponding stimulation of supply. Vastly more money bid for a relatively stable quantity of goods and services causes prices of those goods and services to shoot upward. The value of the dollar—the purchasing power of each unit—plummets. At best, men are no better off than they were previously.

In fact, they are much worse off. For one thing, skyrocketing prices wipe out the value of honest men's life savings. For example, in the United States in 1998 the purchasing power of $100 was less than that of $20 a mere 30 years prior. Economist Thomas Sowell states: "...this means the people who saved money in the 1960s had four-fifths of its value silently stolen from them over the next three decades." In doing so, inflation discourages future savings, engendering a frenzied mentality of "buy now" before prices rise further. During Germany's hyper-inflation of the 1920s, for instance, bar patrons ordered multiple drinks upon entering, beating the minute-by-minute price increases.

In any society, there are overwrought individuals who act out a whim-driven, anti-planning, frenetic lifestyle, splurging today, running up debt, thinking not a whit about tomorrow, concluding in bankruptcy, shattered dreams, or worse. Monetary inflation drives remorselessly rising prices, thereby adding economic incentive to such delirium. The virtue of frugality, of putting away money for one's future—itself an instance of composed rationality, of long-term planning—is severely debilitated. Under inflation, it no longer is profitable to save, because needed or desired goods will be more expensive tomorrow than today.

But inflation wreaks egregiously worse harm. Government's monetary expansion is often part of an "easy money" policy, a desire to expedite businessmen's ability to procure loans, to expand their operations, to hire workers, and to thereby maintain a booming economy. But productive businessmen and responsible individuals generally do not require "easy money" to gain loans, which often goes to marginal producers and "fly-by-night" operators, who proceed to squander the access it provides to capital assets. Inflation is a wasteful policy of irresponsible dissipation.

Worst of all, monetary expansion and ensuing escalating prices undermine confidence in capitalism. When millions of citizens mistakenly presume that capitalism, not statism, is responsible for the dollar's declining value, they are more inclined to abide steadily increasing doses of oppressive statist policies as supposed countermeasures. For example, governments often impose wage-price controls as an alleged anti-inflationary policy.

But restricting rising prices merely tinkers with one effect; it does not efface the underlying cause. The growing quantity of money increases demand for goods relative to their supply. (In fact, it ensures that supply will not increase, because prices cannot rise to a level at which profits grow, spurring increased production.) Now, not everyone able and willing to buy at the fixed prices can procure the items they seek—shortages occur. To combat the state-created shortages, the government imposes rationing, the inevitable consequence of which is everybody making do with less than they otherwise could have—a policy of poverty. The country moves toward statism at an accelerating pace; economic freedom is openly attacked; production and living standards decline.

As pointed out by numerous economists, notably Nobel Laureate, Friedrich Hayek, controls breed increasingly stringent controls, as the state's economic interventions inescapably founder; and it, intoxicated with power—refusing to abdicate—imposes more oppressive edicts seeking to redress the calamities of prior ones.

Inflation is a form of stealth taxation. It is a covert governmental means of increasing its spending capacity without engaging in the politically unpopular act of overtly raising taxes. It is a surreptitious levy imposed on citizens in their role as consumer, not as taxpayer.

Why do governments steal their citizens' wealth in this form? Perhaps they desire increased revenue to build their military and prepare for war—or to promote an "easy money" policy to foment and/or maintain a "boom" economy—or to finance an expanding welfare state, etc. Whatever the state's specific goal, it is insufficiently popular to permit requisite revenue to be raised by means of taxation.

Currently, for example, the multiple Bush/Obama bailouts and stimulus packages, running to trillions of dollars, necessitates fulsome inflation that will be paid for by American citizens—currently and in the future—in the form of steadily rising prices that obliterate the value of their life savings.

The cure for monetary inflation is for politicians to excuse their blustering presence from an economy and permit human beings to once again freely choose their money, i.e., what they will accept as a medium of exchange. In all likelihood, they will choose the metal that, historically, they have generally chosen when left free: gold.

An international gold standard is mankind's primary protection against politicians arbitrarily expanding the money supply. Gold is relatively rare in nature—and its mining generally involves laborious and expensive work—therefore, the money supply grows only gradually. The technological progress of free men leads to an increase in the supply of goods that generally exceeds the increase in the supply of gold. One result is a gradual trending decline of prices, year by year, decade by decade, as free men's production increases—and, consequently, their wealth. Such is exactly what occurred throughout much of the 19th century, including from the 1870s to the 1890s—the Inventive Period.

THE GREAT DEPRESSION

The worst economic calamity wrought by a mixed economy is: depression. Fully socialist regimes, such as Cuba, North Korea, or the former Soviet Union, subsist(ed) in chronic depression. Partly socialist systems, such as Western mixed economies, suffer only periodic depressions. Unrelieved statism engenders unrelieved poverty. A mixture of freedom and statism yields a mixture of prosperity and poverty.

The worst depression of America's history tragically lasted from 1929 to 1946. What were the political-economic conditions of the years immediately preceding it?

Though the United States of the 1920s was a mixed economy, and decidedly less free than during the Inventive Period, it enjoyed vastly greater liberty than after imposition of the New Deal. After World War I, for example, the government had significantly reduced tax rates. President Calvin Coolidge had the good sense to understand that "the chief business of the American people is business"—wisdom for which he has been incessantly assailed by subsequent generations of historians each knowing progressively less of basic economics—and held generally to principles of limited government.

Coolidge retained famed Pittsburgh banker, Andrew Mellon, as Secretary of the Treasury, who slashed taxes across the economic board. Additionally, relative to the New Deal era, governmental regulation of business was less extensive, legislation and court decisions empowering monopolistic labor unions less pervasive, and a welfare state virtually non-existent.

Contrary to common belief, including that of many economists, the prosperity of the 1920s was genuine, not a groundless chimera. The decade was a period of extraordinary economic growth. Invention in the nation flourished—the number of patents issued exceeded prior records. New industries in automobiles, chemicals, appliances, telephones, radios, aircraft, and other fields grew rapidly. The bemused phrase, "what will they think of next?" gained cultural currency in response to ceaseless technological advance. Real wages rose substantially, as did general living standards. Industrial production more than doubled from 1921 to 1929 (+109%). In all of American history, the sole eight-year period of comparable economic growth was during the 1870s—the Inventive Period.

Further, for all of its flaws, the Federal Reserve remained on the gold standard. The dollar retained the same, fixed amount of gold it had for decades—and was freely convertible to any bank or dollar-holder. There was no debasement of the dollar's value. Wholesale and retail prices declined in the years leading up to 1929—meaning the purchasing power of American customers grew.

What factor(s) caused the shattering crash of 1929? More broadly, what were the causes of the Great Depression—of its severity and interminable duration? Business economist, Richard Salsman, points to several critical errors of governmental policy.

First: President Hoover supported the massive Smoot-Hawley Tariff Act: duties would be levied on thousands of imported items of all varieties. The new tariffs imposed an effective tax rate of 60% on more than 3200 products imported into the U.S. Predictably, in retaliation for this quadrupling of import duties, other nations raised tariffs. Numerous countries, for example, substantially raised duties on imported American automobiles. Over the next three years (1930-33), U.S. exports plunged 64%, including farm exports by 60%. Total world trade sunk 61% during those years. Further, the tariff war raised U.S. business costs, thereby depressing profits. As Salsman notes: "That's what the stock market was anticipating in 1929."

Thomas Sowell, widely recognized as one of America's leading economists, wryly makes a similar point: "Economists have long blamed the international trade restrictions around the world for needlessly prolonging the worldwide depression of the 1930s. Economists, however, do not have many votes. Nor do many of the voters know much economics."

Second: for several years leading up to 1929, Congressmen, Federal Reserve officials, and Hoover openly criticized what they believed to be exorbitantly over-priced heights reached by the stock market. Starting in 1928 and continuing throughout 1929, the Fed steadily raised the interest rates it charged for the borrowings of member banks—increasing it from 3.5% to—in August, 1929—6%. This was a punitive policy. For, it limited the funds available for investment, despite the booming productivity of American business.

Throughout 1929, Salsman reports: "the Fed became increasingly obsessed with the stock market and its so-called 'speculative excesses.' The Fed fixated on ways to curb otherwise perfectly legitimate stock gains." In brief, the Fed conducted a relentless campaign against the market's properly bullish attitude that, tragically, contributed to the crash. "Precisely because the gains were extraordinary, rather-ordinary observers could not fully comprehend (or believe) them."

Salsman continues: "Central banking...is a feature of statism—not capitalism." The Federal Reserve System is America's version of it—a government institution wielding control of the banking industry; but through most of the 1920s it exerted relatively little influence—and consequently, wrought little harm. By decade's end, however, the Fed sought to curb the stock market boom, to intercede aggressively and arbitrarily in "matters that previously had been left to market professionals." Now the central bankers controlled the stock market as they thought best. "No fully private, capitalist banking system could ever wield such power—or ever become so arbitrary. Capitalism has no 'official' credit policy to which all must conform—or else suffer."

Prospective investors were now confronted with two harsh truths: money was more difficult to obtain—and governmental policy would no longer support continually rising American productivity. Given ominous governmental policy regarding both trade and finance, it is small wonder investors panicked.

Third: bank failures across America—obliterating the life's savings of millions and wrecking local economies—were a critical part of the statist catastrophe. Almost 10,000 banks failed in America from 1929 to 1933—90% of them in small towns. The prime cause was fear of competition from large financial institutions on the part of many small-town bankers. Unfortunately, fearful rural bankers lobbied successfully in many states for unit banking laws, prohibiting a bank from opening branches. This was classic mixed economy legislation, violating the rights of large banks, ostensibly protecting the "little guy," but thereby limiting many small towns to a single, one-unit bank.

Many such rural banks found it difficult to diversify—both their sources of deposit and portfolio of loans were unrelievedly monochromatic. Often their clients were farmers. When agriculture was hard hit, and farmers withdrew deposits or struggled to repay loans, many one-unit banks could not survive. It is not surprising that historian, Jim Powell, reports: "Almost all the failed banks were in states with unit banking laws that suppressed competition."

By contrast, during the same Depression years, not a single Canadian bank failed. In Canada there were no unit banking laws, and branch banking was legally permitted. Banks, consequently, diversified investments and sources of deposit—and survived when hardship struck specific industries or regions.

Further, the Hoover administration proceeded to impose massive government intervention on the economy, i.e., more germs for the dying man. The president pressured business leaders to maintain high prices and wages—at exactly the moment they needed to decline; and to keep increasing capital outlay—at a time when capital needed to accumulate.

Worst of all, the Smoot-Hawley tariff ushered in a world-wide trend toward protectionism at the exact moment international free trade was most urgently required. By June 1930 unemployment had abated to a level of 6.3%. The ginormous tariff became law that same month. Virtually all of the nation's leading economists urged Hoover to veto it—but he did not.

Thomas Sowell points out that the tariff, highest in more than a century, was "an effort to reduce imports and thus preserve American jobs by having the formerly imported goods produced in the United States instead." In practice, the predictable result was a rise of unemployment rates to 11.6% by November of that year, as the resulting tariff war reduced overseas sales of American goods and raised domestic firms' costs of imports. When combined with other interventionist follies the massive tariff curtailed American business activity, reducing the country to economic prostration during the depression's low ebb annum of 1932.

The United States, history's most capitalist, and consequently, most prosperous nation, now approached socialism's minimalist living standards because it approached socialism's maximalist governmental controls.

It would approach it yet more nearly. Hoover imposed burdensome tax increases, increased government spending for welfare programs, and pushed the federal government's share of GNP upward from 16.4% to 21.5%. In so doing, he laid the basis of FDR's subsequent policies. In one of economic history's tragic ironies, Hoover—an unremitting interventionist—is commonly upheld as an advocate of laissez-faire. Roosevelt's "Brain Trust" knew better. "We didn't admit it at the time," acknowledged FDR advisor, Rexford Tugwell, decades later, "but practically the whole New Deal was extrapolated from programs that Hoover started."

The Hoover/Roosevelt New Deal pushed America remorselessly into the socialist end of the mixed economy—with foreseeable results.

The centerpiece of New Deal legislation, the National Industrial Recovery Act, enacted into law in June of 1933, forced most manufacturing industries into government-controlled cartels. The National Recovery Administration (NRA) imposed regulatory codes and price controls for hundreds of industries that encompassed several million employers and 22 million workers.

Its massive control of prices and terms of sale briefly transformed America into a specifically Fascist-style economic system—one in which private business continued to exist but under massive government control—a system perfect for FDR's hand-picked director, General Hugh "Iron Pants" Johnson, a bullying, self-professed admirer of Mussolini, who threatened to "sock in the nose" anyone failing to comply with NRA dictates. Jack Magid, a New Jersey tailor, for example, was not victimized by an "Iron Pants" Johnson left hook but was jailed for pressing clothes for 35 cents, 5 cents cheaper than permitted by the NRA.

Inevitably, disdainfully, Americans violated such dictatorial laws, forming widespread black markets, impelling NRA crack downs, as its intrusive police thrust into factories like Fascist storm troopers, rounding up employees, interrogating them, seizing the firm's books, and searching for men who committed the heinous, republic-endangering crime of working nights.

The Supreme Court banned the NRA as unconstitutional in 1935, but, chameleon-style, the New Deal persisted in diverse forms. The government tripled taxes, abandoned the gold standard, enacted union-empowering legislation, increased regulation of business, and introduced the Works Progress Administration (WPA), which frequently squandered resources by hiring unemployed laborers to perform uselessly non-productive "make work" schemes.

By late 1937—after more than four years of FDR's programs, and eight years of a combined Hoover/Roosevelt New Deal—unemployment rose in excess of ten million and business activity crumpled to virtually the identical low of 1932. The year 1938 witnessed what economists refer to as " a depression within a depression," as the stock market caved nearly 50% and unemployment climbed to 20%, leaving 11,800,000 out of work, a figure exceeding the 11,385,000 unemployed upon Roosevelt's 1932 election. Indeed, in late-1941, on the eve of America's entry into World War II, ten million Americans were still unemployed.

The war certainly ended unemployment, as roughly 12 million men joined the military forces and booming factories produced armaments for the death struggle against Fascism. But war, under any circumstances, never promotes prosperity. Productive firms manufacture munitions, not consumer goods; food and other indispensables necessarily go to support combatants; otherwise industrious individuals are fighting, not working, often dying by the thousands or even millions; and, if the battles are contested on domestic soil, destroy flourishing farms and industries, as well as hard-working civilians. Domestic shortages are chronic during wartime—and World War II America was no exception.

The sole economic positive of World War II was that it decisively ended the Roosevelt administration's implacably hostile attitude toward business. The anti-capitalist legislation and rhetoric ceased—for the war effort indispensably required America's industries to produce. During the 1930s, businessmen and investors were justifiably scared by the combination of anti-capitalist talk and interventionist action. Public opinion polls in 1939 showed that 54% of Americans and 65% of businessmen believed that the administration's anti-business attitude had severely undermined business confidence and retarded economic recovery.

The war changed all that. Thomas Sowell writes: "In his whimsical way that some found charming, FDR said that 'Dr. New Deal' was replaced by 'Dr. Win-the-War.' The Roosevelt administration abandoned its anti-business stance and the pendulum swung to the other side, with cost-plus government contracts that *guaranteed* business profits to producers of war material."

Full recovery from the Great Depression, i.e., a return to prosperity, was not achieved until after the war. To be blunt, President Truman did not crusade against "economic royalists" and neither the administration's policies nor rhetoric exuded overtones of class warfare. Private investment had dropped precipitously during the 1930s. Now it climbed again. In 1929, for example, gross private investment reached almost 16% of GDP; it fell to less than 2% in 1932; recovered somewhat but did not again reach 16% until 1946. During the 1930s, net private investment declined by $3.1 billion.

It is unfortunately easy to underestimate the importance of the psychological atmosphere created by a government's programs and attitudes. Private investment is the fuel that drives economic progress. It is of the first importance that investors are confident the government will protect, rather than undermine or expropriate their property rights. In an atmosphere fearing a further abrogation of property rights, they will not invest.

The Hoover/Roosevelt restrictions on business limited productivity and, consequently, profit. Related: such policies, especially the overt Fascism of the NRA, combined with FDR's inflammatory rhetoric against those who earned great wealth, understandably frightened hell out of prospective investors, who now held legitimate reasons for clinging to their money.

Economist Lester Chandler makes the point succinctly: "The failure of the New Deal to bring about an adequate revival of private investment is the key to its failure to achieve a complete and self-sustaining recovery of output and employment."

But, in truth, there is a more important factor. Capitalism's greatest material advances are based on inventions and innovations, on breakthroughs in applied science, technology, and industrialization. These require scrupulous implementation of the principle of individual rights that was flagrantly abrogated by the New Deal's unremitting statism. Thomas Edison, for example, often worked 18 hours per day. Would "Iron Pants" Johnson incarcerate him for working nights—or personally sock him in the nose? Is it morally just or economically viable to require the Inventive Period's great innovators and entrepreneurs to beg permission from such as FDR or "Iron Pants" Johnson for their creative work?

Under a mixed economy, the productive process is largely governed by the judgment of such statist politicians and bureaucrats as FDR and General Johnson—not by such thinkers as Edison and other prodigious creators of the Inventive Period. To the degree the men of physical force control an economic system, to that degree the men of creative mind power are shackled.

To that same degree, then, wealth creation is curtailed. If government policy undercuts the cause of wealth—the independent mind—it *ipso facto* weakens the effect. The statist policies of the Hoover/Roosevelt New Deal curbed more than investment; they curbed creativity.

The factors responsible for initiating, aggravating, and extending the worst depression of U.S. history should be noted. Such policies as central government banking in the form of the Federal Reserve System, and its 1920s war against American productivity—the Smoot-Hawley Tariff Act—state laws prohibiting branch banking—the cartelization of American business by the NRA—the abrogation of the gold standard—steadily rising taxes—legislation granting monopolistic status to labor unions, etc., were far-reaching policies of the state. They were universally applicable and legally enforced, as programs responsible for wrecking a nation's entire economy must be.

In the words of economist Lawrence Reed, the Great Depression "was prolonged and exacerbated by a litany of political missteps: trade-crushing tariffs, incentive-sapping taxes, mind-numbing controls on production and competition...It was not a free market which produced 12 years of agony; rather, it was political bungling on a scale as grand as there ever was."

Thomas Sowell reminds us that "during all the previous history of the United States, when the federal government let the economy recover from downturns on its own, no depression was ever as deep or as long lasting as the Great Depression of the 1930s." Based on such factors, economist Gene Smiley concluded: "The 1930s economic crisis is tragic testimony to government interference in market economies." Business economist, Benjamin Anderson, an expert on the Great Depression, put the point more broadly and with greater force: "Governmental economic planning is back seat driving by a man who doesn't know how to drive and who...doesn't know where he wants to go."

Private business(es) on a free market have neither the coercive power nor the extensive influence to reach their tentacles into every arena of an economy, causing widespread bank failures, pervasive monetary mismanagement, production-strangling regulations, eroding investor confidence, and a shattering stock market crash. Mismanaged private companies fail, harming shareholders, customers, suppliers, and employees, but they lack the legal authority and nationwide jurisdiction necessary to profoundly damage the financial status of virtually every man, woman, and child in the country. Only the government possesses sufficient power to wreak such havoc.

THE CURRENT HOUSING BOOM AND BUST

The recent boom and bust of the U.S. housing market, precipitating a crisis among financial institutions, is—from start to end, soup to nuts, root and branch—a mixed economy crisis; engendered by the socialist element of the mixture, impossible under laissez-faire. What were the government's essential missteps?

First: In some parts of the country, notably coastal California, but else-where as well, local governments, ostensibly seeking to preserve greenery, forests, "open space," and the like, passed laws prohibiting development of substantial land areas. The foreseeable result of such restrictive laws was sky-rocketing prices on land open for development.

For example, in 2005, at the height of the housing boom, the ten Ameri-can communities with the largest home price rises over the prior five years were all in California. In the San Francisco area, the average cost of a home was triple the national rate. In San Mateo County—adjacent to San Francis-co—average home prices peaked at over one million dollars in 2007. Califor-nians were often paying mansion prices for modest middle class residences.

And yet, prior to the 1970s, California home prices were not appreciably different than elsewhere in the country. What factor in that state sent home prices through the roof?

Such a phenomenon is unexplainable by simple supply and demand in a free marketplace. For one thing, California population increases during the 1970s, when home prices in the state first became a multiple of the na-tional average, were markedly similar to nationwide percentages (11.9% to 11.5%)—and housing prices in Palo Alto nearly quadrupled while the com-munity's population actually declined. Further, incomes rose during that de-cade at a slower pace in California than they did nationally.

The change that wrought such havoc was political. Thomas Sowell writes: "The decade of the 1970s saw a rapid spread of laws...in California severely restricting the use of land. Often these laws...forbade the building of anything on vast areas of land, in the name of preserving 'open space'... large and growing amounts of land in many coastal California communities became 'open space'—more than half of all the land in San Mateo County, for example." (Unless otherwise noted, all subsequent quotes in this section are from Sowell's excellent 2009 book, *The Housing Boom and Bust*.)

Such politically-created land scarcity sent the price of available land sky-rocketing upward, constituting the prime reason that million dollar price tags came affixed to unprepossessing homes.

Supporting Sowell's claim, an international study shows that an over-whelming preponderance of urban areas worldwide (23 of 26) suffering from such unaffordable housing is plagued by similar land-use restrictions.

By contrast, in Texas, few laws restrict land use. The city of Houston, for example, has not even imposed zoning laws, never mind the stifling restric-tions permeating coastal California. During the 1970s, as Houston incomes rose faster than the national average, the city retained some of the most af-fordable housing in the world. The population of Houston's metropolitan area has more than doubled since 1960—and yet, as stated by Sowell: "Coldwell Banker [a national real estate company] has estimated that a house that costs $155,000 in Houston would cost more than a million dollars in San Jose." In Dallas, as well, persist family incomes higher than the national average side-by-side with housing prices below that average.

A former governor of the Reserve Bank of New Zealand summed up the reality of home prices succinctly: "the affordability of housing is overwhelmingly a function of just one thing, the extent to which governments place artificial restrictions on the supply of residential land."

Second: In their quest for affordable housing, could the politicians simply repeal the arbitrary laws curtailing men's right to develop the land? They could. Did they? They did not.

In classic mixed economy fashion, they heaped on even—and ever more—irrational, rights-violating legislation in a futile quest to remediate the injurious outcome of prior laws.

They misconceived the problem's scope. In fact, nationwide, with the exception of several metropolitan enclaves on the East and West coasts, the cost of home prices declined relative to income. But the politicos saw a national, not a local issue.

Worse, they misconstrued the problem's cause. At the turn of the 20th century, government played little role in the housing market—and few constrictions on building were imposed. The not-so-surprising result was that—in contrast to early 21st century circumstances—Americans paid a lower ratio of their income for housing—roughly 23% in 1901 compared to 33% in 2003. By far the greatest rise in housing expenses, measured either in terms of percent of income or absolute dollar amounts, occurred in locales suffering from severely restrictive land-use legislation. "Where there is the greatest government intervention, housing is least affordable."

In the face of such realities, statist politicians nevertheless insisted that exorbitantly rising home prices reflected a failure of a free market that required legislative intervention to correct.

They proceeded to enact national legislation. In 1977, Congress passed the Community Reinvestment Act (CRA).

The CRA required "each appropriate Federal financial supervisory agency to use its authority when examining financial institutions, to help meet the credit needs of the local communities in which they are chartered consistent with the safe and sound operation of such institutions."

Observe two critical points: 1. Federal regulators were deemed qualified to advise bankers regarding prospective borrowers—those to whom bankers should loan money vouchsafed to them by depositors—2. They were granted legal authority to do so.

How long before federal officials pressured bankers to lend to prospective borrowers of whom they approved—for whichever political expedient— rather than exclusively those the bankers judged sound financial risks? The sole surprise is that it took the better part of two decades.

By the 1990s—in predictable concordance with the altruist-collectivist-socialist axis of a mixed economy farrago—the government, in various forms, under sundry guises, furiously harassed banks to attenuate lending standards for low-income applicants seeking mortgages. Home ownership was the flavor of the month for altruist intellectuals and politicians seeking to combat poverty by means of coercive government welfare programs.

"Because banks are federally regulated enterprises, they need government permission to do many things other businesses do as they see fit." Banks, for example, if found non-compliant with CRA dictates, could be denied the right to open branches, to merge, to sell investment securities, and/or engage in other productive activities eminently within their legitimate moral compass.

The federal government forced banks to lower lending standards.

Consequently, subprime mortgage loans—those made to borrowers who were not sound credit risks—proliferated; the housing market, for years, frenetically boomed; prices roared upward to undreamed-of heights; and banks were temporarily protected—as high-risk borrowers, unable to meet monthly payments, could pay off loans from proceeds of their home's sale.

Key players in this grim charade were "Fannie Mae" (the Federal National Mortgage Association) and "Freddie Mac" (the Federal Home Loan Mortgage Corporation). These are "two government-created, but privately owned, profit-making enterprises that buy mortgages from banks." Banks selling to Fannie and Freddie thereby derive funds on 30 year mortgages without having to wait that duration for homeowners to make all monthly payments.

Fannie and Freddie are classic mixed economy hybrids: responsible to shareholders—but created and backed by the federal government. Investors buy their securities on the implicit assumption that the federal government would not permit them to founder in event of a financial crisis. In the words of the *Wall Street Journal*: "Their profit is privatized but their risk is socialized." In other words, they are a safe financial bet because any monetary gamble they commit—no matter how flagrant—is backed by the federal government's power and willingness to extort taxpayer money to bail out their debt.

As part of the federal government's increasing pressure on financial institutions to lower lending criteria, HUD (Department of Housing and Urban Development) in 1996 mandated that "42 percent of the mortgages bought by Fannie Mae and Freddie Mac were to be financed for people with incomes below the median income in their areas." (How did HUD come up with the arbitrary figure of 42 percent? Did they consult an astrologer? Perhaps it simply seemed reasonable to force-initiating government officials not to coerce lenders to make as much as 43 percent of mortgage loans to individuals with little or no chance of paying them back.)

Under remorseless federal pressure, banks' lending criteria became ever more attenuated. Such "lax lending standards were the foundation for a house of cards that was ready to collapse with a relatively small nudge."

In other words: what would happen if the housing market—for whatever reason—went bust?

The answer was not long forthcoming. In 2004, to combat risk of inflation, the Fed began raising interest rates, which rose to 5.25% in 2006 from a low of one percent earlier. Banks now had to pay more to borrow money and raised their own interest rates on loans, including mortgages.

The short, simple explanation of subsequent events is that many people could no longer meet payments; especially hard hit were those who had financed via subprime borrowing, which often did not constitute 30-year, fixed rate loans but little-or-no down payment, interest-only, adjustable rate mortgages. Foreclosure rates shot up—and banks, which on average, lose an estimated $40,000 per home foreclosed, were financially hammered.

Minority homeowners took out an inordinate share of subprime loans. Thomas Sowell sadly notes: "Both groups [blacks and Latinos] were especially hard hit by the foreclosures that followed the housing bust. So much for the favor being done to minorities."

Economists warned for years that governmental policies had forced financial institutions into an increasingly precarious state. In 2005, for example, American Enterprise Institute scholar, Peter Wallison, stated that if Congress did not alter its policies, "there will be a massive default with huge losses to the taxpayers and systemic effects on the economy." Similarly, *Barron's* magazine chastised the Bush administration's role in the impending cataclysm: "But he [Bush] is exposing taxpayers to tens of billions of dollars of possible losses, luring thousands of moderate-income families into bankruptcy, and risking the destruction of entire neighborhoods..." Alan Greenspan noted: "We are placing the total financial system of the future at a substantial risk." Subsequently, he told the *Financial Times* of London that upheaval in the financial markets was "an accident waiting to happen."

Influential national politicians left the warnings unheeded.

Barney Frank, for example, ranking member and subsequent chairman of the powerful House Financial Services Committee, scoffed at the warnings, stating they "exaggerate[d] a threat of safety" and "conjure up the possibility of serious financial losses to the Treasury, which I do not see." His counterpart in the Senate, Chairman Chris Dodd of the Senate Banking Committee, for years devalued all risks and warnings, claiming that the banks and housing market were, financially, "on a sound footing."

Congressman Frank's remarks upon flouting the warnings were revealing. He worried that such admonitions would engender stricter lending criteria, because "the more pressure there is there, then the less I think we see in terms of affordable housing." *He uttered no rational response to the rather obvious point that forcing banks into extremely low lending standards endangered the financial well-being of the banks—and with it that of the entire U.S. economy. He merely reiterated an altruistic desire to "help" the poor by coercing the sacrifice of the rich.*

After the housing bust, standing amidst the wreckage of America's financial institutions, Congressman Frank made the following observations—and did so with a straight face. He told the *Financial Times* of London that "the subprime crisis demonstrates the serious negative economic and social consequences that result from too little regulation[!]"—that the crisis was precipitated by "bad decisions that were made by people in the private sector," who were actuated by "a conservative philosophy that says the market knows best." Remarks from other members of Congress reflected equally profound understanding.

That politicians often refuse to take responsibility for the failure of their policies, and instead cast aspersions on innocent others, is a truism of mere passing interest in this context. The salient features of the debacle are: 1. This is inveterate mixed economy fubar, fully precipitated by governmental legislation and regulation, impossible under a free banking market, where financiers are reluctant in the extreme to risk depositors' money on those with dubious credit histories.

2. What drives such destructive semi-socialist economic policies is a deeply entrenched altruist ethic that demands sacrifice of the successful to the unsuccessful — leading adherents to conclude, even regarding catastrophic results utterly foreseeable, that the causative laws and underlying intentions were nonetheless a resounding moral triumph. One does not benefit a poor man by granting him a loan he has no chance to repay — and this is one more example in an unceasing succession demonstrating that a self-sacrifice creed is as irremediably impractical as it is hideously immoral.

But the mess was even worse — and government culpability even stronger.

Mid-1990s revisions to the CRA, for the first time, allowed banks to securitize loans containing subprime mortgages. In other words, government legislators and regulators, instead of repealing laws that forced banks into increasingly risky loans, permitted them to save their financial skins (or attempt to) by passing on the risks to investors.

If the government coerced banks to make dangerously bad loans, and refused to belay such practice, its predictable "solution" to the impending financial cataclysm wrought by its laws was to grant banks permission to recoup losses by bilking naïve investors of hard-earned funds. This was fraud, not merely uncriticized, unopposed, and unpunished by legal authorities — but initiated, approved, and morally sanctioned by them.

From *Investor's Business Daily*: "Soon, investment banks such as Bear Stearns were aggressively hawking the securities as 'guaranteed.' Wall Street's pitch was that MBSs [mortgage-backed securities] were as safe as Treasuries, but with a higher yield.

"But they weren't safe. Everyone in the subprime business — from brokers to lenders to banks to investment houses — absolved themselves of responsibility for ensuring the high-risk loans were good.

"The mortgage lenders didn't care, because they were going to sell the loans to banks. The banks didn't care, because they were going to repackage the loans as MBSs. The investors and traders didn't care, because the MBSs were backed by Fannie and Freddie and their implicit government guarantees.

"In other words, nobody up and down the line — from the branch office on main street to the high-rise on Wall Street — analyzed the risk of such ill-advised loans. But why should they? Everybody was just doing what the regulators [and legislators] in Washington wanted them to do."

When the housing market went bust, the Ponzi-scheme imploded, and many investors lost their life savings. Will the bankers and traders who perpetrated such fraud ever be tried, convicted, and incarcerated? Not likely—for they are backed, enabled, and protected by federal regulators and powerful DC lawmakers who initiated, sustained, and carried to grisly conclusion the whole deplorable mess.

Further: if they were tried and convicted, such would constitute mere minimal justice, akin to incarcerating a crime syndicate's subalterns but leaving its capo and lieutenants at liberty and yet wreaking havoc. Who and what principally require indictment and conviction? The members of Congress who aggressed incessantly against the banks; the federal regulators, the lawmakers' compliant lackeys, who enforced Congress's edicts; and, above all—intellectually—an altruist ethic that enshrouds initiation of force and fraud in a mantle of self-righteous nobility.

When government commences to violate individual rights, it necessarily ceases to protect them. When mixed economy legal authorities perpetrate criminal practices—as they do in every law and policy that initiates force against producers—they ineluctably empower the private citizens and companies they control, and with whom they are inherently in collusion, to do likewise.

A mixed economy is grounded in mixed morality; and the altruist-socialist component of the mixture leads to decidedly unmixed—devastatingly dishonest—practices and results.

What is the rational, morally just solution to the problem of affordable housing? The necessary steps should be clear from the earlier contents of this book. An immediate repeal of all laws restricting residential development and the establishment of a free housing market would simultaneously protect the right of individuals to build on land they own, or that they are willing and able to buy—and would result in an increased supply of housing, thereby diminishing its price.

Further, the repeal of all labor legislation and the establishment of a free labor market would, at once, protect the rights of all employers and employees to negotiate voluntarily—and lead to full employment, increased production of goods and services, vastly augmented supply—including of houses—diminishing prices, and rising real wages.

Home ownership for millions did not become reality until the capitalist era—it was (and is) not even a dream for the penurious throngs dying of malnutrition in the pre-and-non capitalist countries and centuries. The system of individual rights liberated and could yet liberate productive human beings to create wealth, including houses; such a system needs only to be politically enacted.

Further still: the system of individual rights includes that to act charitably. An egoist-individualist-capitalist system engenders vast reservoirs of good will. An example of such is Habitat for Humanity, a private organization, founded in America, which by means of voluntary funding and effort builds homes for poor persons the world over.

This author, who has contributed to Habitat, makes a sincere plea to all socialist politicians and regulators, and those who support their policies—and anyone else: if your expressed concern for the poor is sincere, not merely sanctimonious blather that cloaks a lust to enforce sacrifice on successful men, please cease immediately your war against the banks, establish a system of laissez-faire capitalism, stand back and gape at the outpouring productivity—including of affordable housing—and donate your time, wealth, and effort to Habitat for Humanity, and help them build quality homes for poor persons. Use your power of rational persuasion to convince others to voluntarily do the same.

But commence protecting and cease violating the rights of productive individuals.

DEEPER FAILURES OF A MIXED ECONOMY

If socialism, not capitalism, were the political-economic system generating prosperity, then Cuba, North Korea, and the former Soviet Union would be (or have been) wealthy—and the United States and other capitalist (or semi-capitalist) nations poor. But the reverse is manifestly true.

A mixed economy mixes wealth-creating capitalism with poverty-creating socialism. It mixes individual rights with its abrogation. It mixes freedom with statism. It mixes maximal rational planning with minimal such planning. It mixes enhanced value pursuit with suppressed value pursuit. It mixes personal happiness with misery.

Economically: the socialist element of the mixture curtails the productive activities of honest men. For example, the government creates coercive monopolies, thereby legally preventing entrepreneurs from entering a field; its inflationary monetary policies devour the value of honest men's savings; its war against the banks prevents financiers from lending exclusively to productive individuals; a constellation of its onerous interventions causes, deepens, and lengthens depressions; etc. In countless forms, the socialist component of the mixture undermines an economy's productivity and wealth creation. Mankind is poorer because of the wealth both dissipated and uncreated.

Politically: the statist element abrogates individual rights as a principle, as a universal truth, rendering it a dusty artifact of prior ages, a point not to be discussed, much less installed. When individual rights are evicted from the moral forum, what ethical principle prevents the government dictating to publishers and journalists in the manner it does to bankers? Or to novelists, filmmakers, painters, and dramatists? Or to teachers, professors, and scientists? The frighteningly manifest answer is: none.

We, as Americans, are no different in our humanity than the savagely oppressed peoples of North Korea, Myanmar, or Sudan. Our sole protection is Western Civilization's tenuous grasp on reason and its proper political expression: the undying right of a rational individual to his own life, his own mind, and the pursuit of his own happiness. Efface this—and we are no better protected than they. The statist, collectivist element of a mixed economy's political melange, unless ruthlessly excised, ensures steady creep down a parlous incline toward the abyss of totalitarianism.

Morally: the socialist facet of the farrago enshrines altruism, undercutting a proper egoism. In doing so, it casts a glow of luminous virtue over the state's enforced sacrifice of society's most productive individuals, spuriously transforming callous exploitation into upright service in the public welfare. *As National Socialism and Communism drove home to mankind: no atrocity is so colossal that it cannot be justified in name of service to the people. The imprimatur of self-sacrifice cleanses all sins.*

Where altruism is a dominant moral code, the political system devolves inevitably into collectivist totalitarianism. Where it is a pronounced element in a moral mixture, it leads to pronounced elements of coerced service to society, and steadily-increasing abrogation of individual rights.

Epistemologically (the manner in which human beings use their minds to gain knowledge): full socialism makes rational planning fully impossible; partial socialism makes it merely partially impossible.

To the extent the government controls an economy, to this degree it is run by men who initiate force against productive citizens under its legal jurisdiction—not by men who create values brought to a competitive marketplace for the voluntary consideration of prospective customers.

Government control places human economic relationships in the hands of the men of force—not the men of reason.

Men of force issue arbitrary edicts, e.g., 42% of mortgages bought by Fannie Mae and Freddie Mac must be financed for people with incomes below the median in their locales—not rational judgments, e.g., it is sound banking practice to loan money exclusively to individuals whose credit and/or work history demonstrates a proven ability to pay it back.

To the degree the government runs an economy, a small cadre of legislators and regulators "plan"; and to that degree, tens of millions of individuals, their rights now abrogated, their knowledge and expertise rendered inapplicable, are excluded from the planning process—e.g., bankers and their depositors, who would never countenance diminished lending standards.

Full socialism represents a full war against the mind; partial socialism, partial war against it. Full socialism, waging all-out war against man's survival instrument, ensures that many men do not survive; half-socialism, waging only half-war, ensures that those who do survive do so at diminished living standards.

Capitalism is individual rights, it is freedom—and freedom has no down side. The question, for all rational human beings to ponder and answer in their own consciences is: why curtail it with elements of statism and poverty?

Epilogue
A Modern Proposal

In 1729, the Anglo-Irish writer, Jonathan Swift, published his essay, "A Modest Proposal," in which he suggested that destitute Ireland might ease its poverty by selling children as food for wealthy English aristocrats. The essay was a brilliant exercise in sustained literary irony.

This author's proposal, by contrast, is fully earnest. In several parts:

1. Let the United States move to full laissez-faire capitalism, assiduously protecting individual rights in all arenas of human life, including personal morality, as well as economics.

2. Let every other nation, without exception, if they so choose, move to partial socialism (full socialism is a horror not to be wished on any human being), to whatever degree each country's populace wishes.

3. Open the borders of all countries, so that every honest person—but not criminals or terrorists—can emigrate to the land he prefers.

4. Over a period of decades, even centuries, conduct a "Great Laboratory," honestly studying the progress of each nation, emigration patterns between nations, and levels of fulfillment/happiness among individual citizens of each nation.

The world's governments have far too little respect for individual rights and freedom to ever institute such a policy—although they could and should. Rational individuals must content themselves with merely a striking thought experiment.

Several predictions: Emigration will run overwhelmingly to capitalist

America, away from the semi-socialist rest of the world—because the "common man" overwhelmingly prefers freedom and prosperity to statism and poverty. "The Brain Drain" will continue to vastly favor America, as many of the brightest, most educated, and most skilled men and women opt for freedom. One virtue of such a global agreement is that it protects each individual's right to reside under the political-economic system he deems, by means of his own judgment, to embody moral rectitude and economic productiveness.

Further: values are the meaning of life. The freest country protects each man's right to pursue his cherished personal values without hindrance from others. It follows logically that an enormous preponderance of human beings will be happiest in the freest nation. Therefore, psychologists, honestly researching happiness quotients, will find vastly greater happiness under freedom than under statism—and, as one consequence, emigration patterns will continue to reflect this.

Some might think that the massive welfare states of the semi-socialist nations are more attractive than the protection of individual rights offered by capitalism. Several points in response: 1. Under the world freedom of this proposal all who do are at liberty to reside in such countries. 2. The diminished sense of personal responsibility to which paternalistic care inevitably leads—and the ensuing decline of productivity—will be profoundly unattractive to mankind's most conscientious members—those who think independently and work productively. Under free emigration policies, they will flock to America—as they always have. 3. How much time before the semi-socialist welfare states are left with a preponderance of those who prefer to a self-supporting existence one parasitical off of productive men and women robbed by the government?

After this book's previous discussions, it should go without saying that the free nation's creation of wealth will vastly exceed that of the semi-controlled ones. It is to be hoped that America's burgeoning prosperity, a direct consequence of her diligent allegiance to individual rights, would then inspire movements toward similar freedom in the world's other nations.

This book's theme is that individual rights, fully implemented under a system of laissez-faire, protects all men, without exception, and thereby maximizes human prosperity; and that its abrogation, to the degree it is rescinded, violates the rights of all honest men, and curtails their capacity to attain flourishing life.

Capitalism Unbound concludes with a proposal to socialist intellectuals: if you can refute the theme of this book, proceed to do so. If you cannot, cease gibbering in support of socialism.

In order to succeed, logic requires you to relinquish ad hominem attacks, half-truths, and emotionalist hysteria, and make your case exclusively on a foundation of facts and rational argumentation based in them.

Under such stringent intellectual rules, it is strongly to be doubted that any socialist writer will even attempt a refutation—for they know it cannot be done.